WHAT TO DO WITH PROPHECY

A Comprehensive Guide to How to Steward a Prophetic Word

DAVID SOLA OLUDOYI

SHINING LIGHT GROUP

Contents

This book is dedicated to the Holy Spirit.

To all the Prophets in this age.

To all who desire to function in the prophetic ministry.

Acknowledgements

Awesome gratitude to the Almighty God for the privilege to write this book, despite very challenging and demanding circumstances.

I must appreciate my deceased parents who first introduced me to the power and efficacy of the prophetic. I am proud to say my life is proof that prophecies do come to pass.

I am sincerely grateful for all the members of my local assembly, *Royal Connections*, London, England. To the staff at *Royal Connections* office, thank you for standing with me and running with the vision.

Immense thanks to all my colleagues in ministry and friends who have stood with me in this prophetic journey.

It is crucial that I appreciate the amazing role played by Dr Babatunde Pascal Ojewunmi. Your thoughts, research, and suggestions were invaluable.

I appreciate Pastor Adeleke Sanusi, the Continental

Overseer of *The Redeemed Christian Church of God*, Europe Continent 9, despite very difficult schedule agreed to write the foreword to this book, and professor Babatunde Adedibu for his commendation of the book.

To my dearest wife and partner in the journey of life thank you for your unwavering support.

To my amazing children, Sade & Sam, Enoch-David, Mary-Grace and my grandson Malachi, you are products of prophecies, and your destinies are riding on the wings of prophecies.

Let's go explore what to do with prophecies.

Foreword

Without any doubt, this is a very timely book coming at a time when the all-important subject of prophecy is either not taken seriously by the church or is distorted by various winds of doctrine permeating these end times. Sadly, many are being blown away from the truth by the religious bigotry attacking the church of Christ.

Dr. Oludoyi has, in this book, given us a very simple yet profound understanding of all we need to know from Scripture about prophets, prophecy, and prophesying. The reader is made to appreciate and value the divine significance of this subject from sound scriptural standpoint. This book represents a much-needed deliverance from ignorance, misconceptions, misgivings, misrepresentations, and misapplications that have plagued this God-given gift to the church and humanity.

The reader will no doubt be blessed with the valuable insights given by the author on the purpose of prophecy as God's way of sending encouragement, exhortation, comfort, warning, guidance, revelations, and confirmation of His plans to individuals, families, churches, communities, cities, and nations.

This book is full of practical steps and actions the reader can take to better understand, appreciate, appropriate, and apply prophetic messages to assess the wonders of God to humanity. To say the least, the author has lifted and eradicated the veil of darkness and blindness the enemy has used to undermine this valuable gift to the church.

The book contains many testimonies of real people who have received prophecies and taken the right approach to appropriate them, hence getting desired miraculous break-throughs and turnarounds. I personally can relate to the truth in this book especially while reading the testimonies of those who have benefited from the ministry of prophecy.

I have no hesitation in commending *What To Do With Prophecy* to everyone, being in no doubt that you will be mightily blessed; you will understand the subject better; you will overcome every misconception about the subject; you will discover your own inner spiritual gifts, and your faith will leap up to the point that it will be said of you as it was said of Mary: *"Blessed is she who believed, for there will be a fulfilment of those things which were told her from the Lord"* (Luke 1:45).

Pastor Leke Sanusi

Continental Overseer Europe Continent 9
The Redeemed Christian Church of God

Endorsement

Today, with the convulsive and unpredictable course of world events, the argument of "What to Do with Prophecy?" must be increasingly pressing. Drawing upon biblical sources, the book also explains that 'the field of prophecy' can 'help us trace out the places where understanding breaks down.' It is a 'mark of intellectual health' that these places are identified, though it is another matter to insist on what should be clearly obvious.

Perhaps, the most interesting part of the book is his discussion of the moral questions that go with the act of prophesying: the strengths and weaknesses of such a role, especially how far the interpreter should go with the prophecy and how much should be disclosed to the person receiving it. Appropriately enough, this all ties in to his subsequent reflections on the moral implications of listening to seers and what one should do with their prophetic vision. His more general conclusions on whether and how one should or could make use of prophecies are also well-balanced.

It's also good at dissecting how these visions have played a role in decision-making, be it in private lives, governments, religious institutions – all of them specific times and places where the appeal of prophecy as a sort of guiding light, as a tool for living, is often pursued with little critical examination.

To sum up: *What to Do with Prophecy* provides an impressive and thought-provoking guide to various aspects of the practice of prophecy. It is a valuable and mind-opening book. I recommend it without reservation.

Prof. Babatunde Adedibu

Professor Extraordinary

Professor of Church History and Missiology

Head, Department of Religious Studies and Philosophy,

Redeemer's University, Ede Osun State

Introduction

Despise not prophesyings.

1 Thessalonians 5:20

And so we have the prophetic word confirmed, which you do well to heed as a light that shines in a dark place, until the day dawns and the morning star rises in your hearts; knowing this first, that no prophecy of Scripture is of any private interpretation, for prophecy never came by the will of man, but holy men of God spoke as they were moved by the Holy Spirit.

2 Peter 1:19-21

The concept of prophecy, especially within Christianity, has indeed faced various challenges and misuses throughout history. While the term "bastardised" may be strong, it is fair to say that the practice and understanding of prophecy have faced distortion, misapplication, and controversy over time. For example, I outline below a few circumstances in which prophecy has faced negative concerns:

At times, individuals or groups may misinterpret or exploit prophetic messages for personal gain or manipulation. Such misuse undermines the credibility and true purpose of prophecy. In certain instances, prophecy has been commercialised or treated as entertainment rather than a serious spiritual practice, which can diminish its significance and authenticity.

Prophecy has been shaped by various cultural and historical contexts, which can lead to variations and sometimes distortions of its original biblical intent. Throughout history, some have claimed to speak prophetically but delivered messages inconsistent with biblical teachings or found to be deceitful. This has led to scepticism and confusion about authentic prophetic voices. Different Christian denominations and traditions interpret prophecy differently, leading to varied practices and understandings that can sometimes result in confusion or division.

While these issues have affected the perception and practice of prophecy, it is important to distinguish between these distortions and the authentic, biblically grounded prophetic messages that are intended to guide, encourage, and build up the church. It is also important to acknowledge that in the Christian faith, prophecy is a powerful way God speaks to us, guiding and revealing His will. *What to Do with Prophecy* provides an in-depth evaluation of how to understand, interpret, and apply these divine messages in our everyday lives. This book explores the role of prophecy within the church and offers practical guidance on how individuals can engage with and respond to prophetic messages in a meaningful way.

Chapter one aims to offer a detailed exploration of prophecy's role across both testaments, setting a foundation for understanding its purpose and impact in the life of believers and the church. Chapter two, divided into three sections, focuses on different aspects of how prophecy functions within the church community. Through these sections, I aim to provide a comprehensive understanding of the multifaceted role of prophecy, highlighting its contributions to spiritual growth, unity, and leadership.

In Chapter three, I guide you through the essential steps to take when a prophetic word is spoken over your life. Prophecy is a powerful gift that can provide divine direction, but it requires more than just hearing - it calls for an active and thoughtful response. Simply receiving a word is not enough; you need to engage with it intentionally to see it come to fruition.

Chapter four serves as a comprehensive roadmap for believers who are seeking to see the prophetic words spoken over their lives come to fruition. It outlines the essential steps required to move from receiving a prophecy to experiencing its fulfilment, ensuring that believers actively participate in the process with faith, patience, and obedience.

Chapter five, delves into the real-world impact of

engaging with prophecy, exploring how it shapes both individual lives and entire communities. When believers receive and act on prophetic words with faith, the results are often transformative, leading to lasting change.

In chapter six, you will discover practical ways to handle the challenging period when the fulfilment of a prophetic word seems delayed.

In the final chapter, I conclude by emphasising the vital and multifaceted role of prophecy in our Christian journey and community. Prophecy connects us with God's purposes, whether those purposes are revealed in an instant or unfold gradually over time. Through understanding, discerning, and responding to prophetic messages, we experience profound spiritual growth and contribute to the strengthening of the church. As 2 Peter 1:19 reminds us, the prophetic word serves as a guiding light in our lives. Therefore, with humility, faith, and discernment, we can align ourselves more closely with God and advance His purposes in both our personal lives and the broader world.

Chapter One

Understanding Prophecy

Prophecy is a vital and multifaceted component of the Christian faith, serving as a means of communication between God and His people. It is essential to grasp both the definition and purpose of prophecy to fully appreciate its role in the life of the church and individual believers.

> *But he who prophesies speaks edification and exhortation and comfort to men. He who speaks in a tongue edifies himself, but he who prophesies edifies the church. I wish you all spoke with tongues, but even more that you prophesied; for he who prophesies is greater than he who speaks with tongues, unless indeed he interprets, that the church may receive edification.*
>
> *1 Corinthians 14:3-5*

> *And He Himself gave some to be apostles, some prophets, some evangelists, and some pastors and teachers, for the equipping of the saints for the work of ministry, for the edifying of the body of Christ.*
>
> **Ephesians 4:11-12**

Prophets, Prophecies, and Prophesyings

Let us define these three key concepts—Prophets, Prophecies, and Prophesyings. These fundamental terms are central to the themes of this book. Gaining a clear understanding of these concepts early on will enhance your ability to fully engage with and benefit from the insights offered throughout this book.

Prophets

Prophets are individuals called by God to act as His spokespersons. They receive divine messages and communicate them to people. Their role is critical in guiding, instructing, and sometimes correcting individuals or entire nations according to God's will. For example, Moses, often considered the greatest prophet, received direct communication from God and led the Israelites out of Egypt (Deuteronomy 34:10). Isaiah was known for his prophecies concerning the coming Messiah and Israel's future (Isaiah 7:14; 9:6). Jeremiah delivered messages of warning and hope to Israel, especially during Judah's difficult times (Jeremiah 1:4-10; 29:11).

In their role and purpose, these prophets are divinely appointed to reveal God's plans, confront sin, offer hope, and guide people. Their messages provide divine insight and help align individuals and nations with God's purposes.

Prophecies

Prophecies are the specific messages or revelations given by God through prophets. These messages can predict future events, reveal divine truths, or offer guidance and instructions for current situations. For example, the following prophecy by Isaiah predicted the miraculous birth of Jesus Christ: *"Therefore the Lord Himself will give you a sign: Behold, the virgin shall conceive and bear a Son, and shall call His name Immanuel"* (Isaiah 7:14).

The book of revelation is a prophecy that reveals the events leading to the end times and Christ's ultimate victory. The entire book is *"the revelation of Jesus Christ, which God gave Him to show His servants — things which must shortly take place"* (Revelation 1:1). In purpose and impact, these prophecies are designed to reveal God's plans, offer guidance, provide warnings, or encourage people. They help prepare individuals and communities for future events and align them with divine intentions.

Prophesyings

Prophesyings refer to the act of delivering prophetic messages. This term encompasses the practice of speaking forth divine revelations, predictions, or instructions. In 1 Corinthians 14:1, Paul admonishes believers to *"Pursue love, and desire spiritual gifts, but especially that you may prophesy."* In this verse, Paul encourages believers to seek the gift of prophecy, highlighting its importance for church edification.

The scriptures also declare that *"And it shall come to pass in the last days, says God, That I will pour out of My Spirit on all flesh; your sons and your daughters shall prophesy, your young men shall see visions, your old men shall dream dreams"* (Acts 2:17-18). This passage describes the widespread practice of prophesying in the last days because of the Holy Spirit's outpouring.

In purpose and function, prophesyings involve delivering divine messages and can occur in various settings such as worship services or personal experiences. They are meant to build up, encourage, and provide insight to believers.

It is important that I address an important question while I am still here. Reflecting on Acts 2:17-18, the passage expresses the widespread practice of prophesying as inspired by the outpouring of the Holy Spirit upon all flesh. The question is, can individuals without a title of a prophet prophesy in different situations and circumstances?

Individuals can indeed operate in a prophetic capacity within their own situations and circumstances, though this is often through a manifestation of spiritual gifts and sensitivity to God's leading rather than a formal prophetic office. By aligning your actions and words with biblical principles and seeking to discern God's will, you can function prophetically in personal, contextual and community settings.

God's people can embody prophetic truths through their actions and words, influencing those around them and reflecting God's guidance in practical ways (Matthew 5:14-16). They can also have a heightened awareness of God's leading in personal or communal matters, guiding others with wisdom and insight.

We are encouraged in scripture to provide prophetic messages that uplift and comfort others in our community. For instance, someone might sense a need to offer a word of encouragement during a difficult time, aligning with the purpose of exhortatory prophecy (1 Corinthians 14:3). I will explain what exhortatory prophecy means in detail when I discuss different types of prophecies. Personal prophecies can provide direction or insight into decisions that align with biblical teaching, helping others navigate their circumstances (Acts 21:10-11).

Contextual Prophetic Influence

In specific situations, individuals may function prophetically by addressing current issues or providing insights relevant to their circumstances. This includes speaking truth in a way that aligns with God's will and divine insight.

> *"Then one of them, named Agabus, stood up and showed by the Spirit that there was going to be a great famine throughout all the world, which also happened in the days of Claudius Caesar."*

Acts 11:28

Agabus, a member of the early church, provided a prophetic message about a future famine, demonstrating how individual insights can impact a community. Indeed, Holy Spirit can inspire individuals to receive and share insights into God's plans or revelations about current or future events (Revelation 1:1). These insights are meant to inform and guide others according to God's will.

The Holy Spirit can inspire you to address issues or behaviours in your community, calling for repentance or realignment with biblical principles (Jeremiah 1:10).

Community and Church Settings

Within a church or community, believers can exercise prophetic gifts by speaking into the life of the church or fellowship, offering divine guidance or correction as led by the Holy Spirit. Paul, in 1 Thessalonians 5:20, instructs believers to respect and value prophetic messages within the church community, indicating that prophecy is relevant for communal life. An individual's prophetic contributions can build up the church, offer encouragement, and help direct collective efforts (1 Corinthians 14:4). An individual may offer prophetic insights that aid in making decisions, such as appointing leaders or planning ministry activities (Acts 13:2-3).

Understanding 4 Types of Prophecies

1. Predictive Prophecy

Predictive prophecy involves proclaiming events that will occur in the future. These prophecies provide a glimpse into what God has planned, often with specific details. Predictive prophecies reaffirm God's control over history provides believers with assurance about the future. They call for faith and preparation, showing that God's plans are certain and will come to pass.

2. Revelatory Prophecy

Revelatory prophecy reveals new, previously unknown insights about God's character, His will, or His plans. This type of prophecy helps to uncover divine mysteries and deepen understanding. Revelatory prophecy exposes hidden truths, often leading individuals to recognise God's presence and power. Revelatory prophecies enhance believers' understanding of divine truth and God's plans, enriching their spiritual knowledge and guiding their actions in accordance with God's will.

> *"But if all prophesy, and an unbeliever or an uninformed person comes in, he is convinced by all, he is convicted by all. And thus the secrets of his heart are revealed; and so, falling down on his face, he will worship God and report that God is truly among you."*

> **1 Corinthians 14:24-25**

> *"The revelation of Jesus Christ, which God gave Him to show His servants - things which must shortly take place. And He sent and signified it by His angel to His servant John."*

> **Revelation 1:1-2**

The book of Revelation contains revelatory prophecies about the end times and the ultimate victory of Christ, providing insight into future events and spiritual realities.

3. Exhortatory Prophecy

Exhortatory prophecy focuses on encouragement, comfort, and urging people towards righteous living. It often includes calls to repentance and reassurance of God's promises. Exhortatory prophecies provide support and encouragement, helping believers navigate life's challenges with assurance and trust in God's guidance.

"But he who prophesies speaks edification and exhortation and comfort to men."

1 Corinthians 14:3

This type of prophecy is meant to build up the church, offering hope and encouragement, especially in times of difficulty.

"And as we stayed many days, a certain prophet named Agabus came down from Judea. When he had come to us, he took Paul's belt, bound his own hands and feet, and said, 'Thus says the Holy Spirit, "So shall the Jews at Jerusalem bind the man who owns this belt, and deliver him into the hands of the Gentiles."

Acts 21:10-11

Agabus' prophecy prepared Paul for the trials he would face, offering him insight and encouragement to face the future with faith.

4. Conditional Prophecy

Conditional prophecies outline outcomes based on human responses to God's commands. These prophecies show how God's plans can change depending on whether people heed or ignore His instructions.

And Jonah began to enter the city on the first day's walk. Then he cried out and said, 'Yet forty days, and Nineveh shall be overthrown!

Jonah 3:4

The prophecy of Nineveh's destruction was conditional on their repentance. Their change of heart spared the city from judgment (Jonah 3:10).

> *The instant I speak concerning a nation and concerning a kingdom, to pluck up, to pull down, and to destroy it, if that nation against whom I have spoken turns from its evil, I will relent of the disaster that I thought to bring upon it. And the instant I speak concerning a nation and concerning a kingdom, to build and to plant it, if it does evil in My sight so that it does not obey My voice, then I will relent concerning the good with which I said I would benefit it."*

> *Jeremiah 18:7-10*

This passage emphasises that God's prophetic declarations are conditional on the responses of nations or individuals. Conditional prophecies highlight the importance of obedience and repentance. They demonstrate that human choices impact how God's plans unfold and encourage people to align with His will.

Prophetic Actions

Prophetic actions involve symbolic acts performed by prophets to illustrate or reinforce a divine message. These actions are visual demonstrations of God's messages.

> *You also, son of man, take a clay tablet and lay it before you, and portray on it a city, Jerusalem. Lay siege against it, build a siege wall against it, and heap up a mound against it; set camps against it*

also, and place battering rams against it all around.

Ezekiel 4:1-3

Ezekiel's symbolic act of portraying the siege of Jerusalem visually communicated the impending judgment upon the city.

"When the Lord began to speak by Hosea, the Lord said to Hosea: *'Go, take yourself a wife of harlotry and children of harlotry, for the land has committed great harlotry by departing from the Lord.'* So, he went and took Gomer the daughter of Diblaim, and she conceived and bore him a son." Hosea's marriage to Gomer was a living parable representing Israel's unfaithfulness to God and His persistent love for them. Prophetic actions serve to make divine messages more impactful and memorable. They provide a tangible representation of God's messages and help believers grasp complex spiritual truths.

Prophecy in the Life of the Believer and the Church

Prophecies offer divine guidance, helping believers and the church make decisions aligned with God's will. For example, prophetic guidance in the early church helped in decisions like appointing elders and directing missionary work (Acts 13:2-3).

Prophecies provide reassurance and hope, especially during challenging times. The comfort found in prophecy, such as the promise of Christ's return (John 14:3), strengthens believers' faith. Prophecy unveils aspects of God's plans and purposes, enhancing understanding. The revelation of Jesus' mission through prophetic messages (Luke 24:27) deepens believers' grasp of divine intent.

When prophecies are fulfilled, they build trust in God and His promises. Seeing prophecies come to pass, like the predictions about Jesus' life and resurrection (Matthew 26:56), reinforces believers' confidence in God's faithfulness. Prophecies can serve as a call to repentance and correction. For example, Jonah's message to Nineveh led to their repentance and spared them from destruction (Jonah 3:10).

Prophecies contribute to the church's edification, offering wisdom, encouragement, and direction. This strengthens the church's mission and unity (1 Corinthians 14:4).

Prophecies affirm God's control over history and His commitment to His promises. They reveal that God's plans are unchanging and certain, encouraging believers to trust in His overarching sovereignty (Isaiah 46:10).

New Testament Prophetic Ministry

The New Testament represents a significant continuation and expansion of prophetic ministry, as the early Christian community experienced a profound movement of the Holy Spirit.

But this is what was spoken by the prophet Joel: 'And it shall come to pass in the last days, says God, That I will pour out of My Spirit on all flesh; Your sons and your daughters shall prophesy, your young men shall see visions, your old men shall dream dreams. And on My menservants and on My maidservants, I will pour out My Spirit in those days; And they shall prophesy.'

Acts 2:16-18

The day of Pentecost marked a pivotal moment in Christian history when the Holy Spirit descended upon the apostles, enabling them to speak in various tongues and prophesy. This event signified the beginning of a new era where the Spirit's gifts, including prophecy, became widely accessible to all believers, transcending age, gender, and social status. Peter's sermon in Acts 2 underscores that what was happening was a direct fulfilment of Joel's prophecy, indicating the dawn of the last days and the widespread availability of prophetic gifts.

The early church recognised the importance of prophets and prophetic ministry as integral to its structure and function. 1 Corinthians 12:28 notes, *"And God has appointed these in the church: first apostles, second prophets, third teachers, after that is miracles, then gifts of healings, helps, administrations, varieties of tongues."*

Prophets in the early church served multiple roles. God used them to give direction for the church. For instance, in Acts 13:1-3, prophets and teachers in the church at Antioch received a prophetic word to set apart Barnabas and Saul (Paul) for missionary work.

Prophetic words often confirmed God's will and provided encouragement. In Acts 15:32, Judas and Silas, themselves prophets, encouraged and strengthened the believers with many words. Prophets also warned of impending events. In Acts 21:10-14, the prophet Agabus predicted Paul's imprisonment, preparing Paul and the church for what lay ahead.

The book of Revelation stands as a testament to the prophetic revelations received by John, the apostle. John's visions, received while exiled on the island of Patmos, encompass a range of prophetic insights concerning the end times, the ultimate triumph of Christ, and the establishment of God's kingdom. They provide hope and encouragement to believers facing persecution, assuring them of Christ's eventual victory. They warn of the consequences of sin and the judgment to come. They offer specific instructions for the seven churches, addressing their unique situations and calling them to faithfulness.

The New Testament illustrates a dynamic and expansive view of prophetic ministry, demonstrating its crucial role in guiding, encouraging, and instructing the early Christian community. From the fulfilment of Joel's prophecy on Pentecost to the active participation of prophets in church life and the profound revelations given to John, prophecy continues to be a vital aspect of Christian faith and practice.

Understanding this continuation and expansion helps us as believers to appreciate the depth and breadth of God's communication through prophetic means, encouraging us to be open to the Spirit's guidance in our lives.

Chapter Two

The Role of Prophecy
in the Church

Prophecy plays a vital role in the life of the church, serving as a means of building up the body of Christ, offering encouragement, and guiding church leadership. Through the act of prophesying, the church community is edified and strengthened in its collective faith.

> *"How is it then, brethren? Whenever you come together, each of you has a psalm, has a teaching, has a tongue, has a revelation, has an interpretation. Let all things be done for edification."*
>
> **1 Corinthians 14:26**

> *"but, speaking the truth in love, may grow up in all things into Him who is the head—Christ— from whom the whole body, joined and knit together by what every joint supplies, according to the effective working by which every part does its share, causes growth of the body for the edifying of itself in love."*
>
> **Ephesians 4:15-16**

In his letters to the Corinthians and the Ephesians, the apostle Paul clearly highlights the significance and proper role of prophesying within the church. By looking at 1 Corinthians 14:26 and Ephesians 4:15-16, we can see how prophesying plays a vital part in the spiritual growth and unity of the body of Christ. Paul underscores that every aspect of a church gathering, including prophesying, should aim to build up the church. As we discussed in chapter 1, where we explored the roles of prophets, prophecies, and prophesyings, prophesying involves delivering messages inspired by the Holy Spirit. These messages are meant to build up, encourage, and comfort the congregation. It is a way for God to speak directly to His people, providing essential insight and guidance for their spiritual development and wellbeing.

Spiritual Growth Through Prophecy

Prophecy reveals God's will and purpose for individuals and the church. This revelation helps believers align their lives with God's desires, fostering spiritual maturity. By understanding God's plans through prophecy, believers deepen their relationship with Him, learning to trust and obey His guidance. Romans 12:6 says, *"Having then gifts differing according to the grace that is given to us, let us use them: if prophecy, let us prophesy in proportion to our faith."*

Prophetic messages frequently include correction and guidance, helping believers stay on the right path. When the church or individuals stray, prophecy serves as a divine reminder of God's standards, prompting repentance and realignment with biblical principles. In 2 Timothy 3:16, it is written, *"All Scripture is given by inspiration of God, and is profitable for doctrine, for reproof, for correction, for instruction in righteousness."*

Receiving a prophetic word that speaks directly to personal circumstances can significantly strengthen faith. When believers witness prophetic words coming to pass, it builds their confidence in God's omniscience and omnipotence, encouraging them to rely more fully on Him. Hebrews 11:1 reminds us, *"Now faith is the substance of things hoped for, the evidence of things not seen."*

Promoting Unity in the Church Through Prophecy

Prophecy fosters a sense of community within the church. When shared, prophetic messages often address communal concerns and encourage collective action, thus strengthening the bonds between members. Shared experiences of receiving and witnessing the fulfilment of prophecy unify believers in their faith journey. Acts 2:44-47 illustrates this community spirit: *"Now all who believed were together, and had all things in common, and sold their possessions and goods, and divided them among all, as anyone had need."*

The New Testament model of church life, as seen in 1 Corinthians 14:26, involves every member participating and contributing their spiritual gifts for the common good: *"How is it then, brethren? Whenever you come together, each of you has a psalm, has a teaching, has a tongue, has a revelation, has an interpretation. Let all things be done for edification."* Prophecy encourages this participatory model by valuing the contributions of all members, promoting a sense of belonging and mutual respect.

Prophecy, when exercised in love and humility, contributes to the mutual edification of the church. As believers share prophetic messages, they build each other up, providing support and encouragement. This reciprocal edification strengthens the entire church body as each member grows in their spiritual walk and contributes to the growth of others. Ephesians 4:15-16 says, *"but, speaking the truth in love, may grow up in all things into Him who is the head—Christ—from whom the whole body, joined and knit together by what every joint supplies, according to the effective working by which every part does its share, causes growth of the body for the edifying of itself in love."*

Orderly worship is crucial for the proper functioning of prophetic gifts. Paul emphasises the need for order in the exercise of spiritual gifts, including prophecy, to ensure that all things are done decently and in order (1 Corinthians 14:40). This orderliness prevents chaos and confusion, making it easier for the congregation to receive and respond to prophetic messages effectively.

Prophecy helps maintain doctrinal purity by providing divine insight and correction. When false teachings or practices arise, prophetic messages can expose these errors and call the church back to biblical truth. This safeguarding of doctrine is essential for preserving the unity of the faith (Ephesians 4:13).

Importance of Orderly Worship and Mutual Edification

Paul's instructions in 1 Corinthians 14:26-33 highlight the importance of a structured approach to using spiritual gifts, including prophecy. Each member's contribution should be made in an orderly fashion to ensure clarity and edification. This structure allows the Holy Spirit to work through each member without causing confusion or disruption.

Orderly worship ensures that no single gift or individual dominates the gathering. This balance allows for a more holistic approach to worship and edification, where teaching, prophecy, singing, and other gifts all contribute to the spiritual well-being of the church. Romans 12:4-6 explains, *"For as we have many members in one body, but all the members do not have the same function, so we, being many, are one body in Christ, and individually members of one another. Having then gifts differing according to the grace that is given to us, let us use them."*

Orderly worship fosters an environment of mutual respect and love. When everyone is given the opportunity to contribute their gifts in an orderly manner, it demonstrates that each member is valued and respected. This atmosphere of love and respect is crucial for the healthy functioning of the church body (Ephesians 4:16).

Paul's exhortation to speak the truth in love (Ephesians 4:15) highlights the importance of love in the exercise of spiritual gifts. Prophetic messages should be delivered with a heart of love, aiming to build up rather than tear down. This loving approach ensures that prophecy contributes to the overall growth and unity of the church.

3 Characteristics of Prophecy

"But he who prophesies speaks edification and exhortation and comfort to men."

1 Corinthians 14:3

"Now Judas and Silas, themselves being prophets also, exhorted and strengthened the brethren with many words."

Acts 15:32

In 1 Corinthians 14:3, Paul highlights the essential purpose of prophecy in the church: to edify, exhort, and comfort. *Edification* means building up the church by strengthening the faith and spiritual understanding of its members. *Exhortation* is about encouraging believers to live out their faith more fully and to stay committed to God. *Comfort* provides solace and reassurance to those who are struggling or in distress. So, prophecy is a key tool for spiritual growth and support within the Christian community.

Acts 15:32 gives us a real-life example of how prophecy works in the church. Judas and Silas, both prophets, used their gifts to encourage and strengthen the believers. This perfectly aligns with Paul's teaching in 1 Corinthians, showing that prophecy is not just about predicting the future. It is about speaking God's truth to uplift and build up the church. Their prophetic words provided guidance, encouragement, and reinforcement of faith, highlighting the crucial role of prophecy in maintaining the unity and health of the early Christian community.

These aspects of prophecy are crucial for both individual growth and the wellbeing of the church community. Let us explore how prophecy serves these purposes and look at some biblical examples where prophetic words have provided strength and support.

1. Edification

Prophecy encourages believers by helping them persevere and stay committed to their faith. For instance, in Acts 23:11, the Lord reassures Paul with a prophetic message: *"Be of good cheer, Paul; for as you have testified for Me in Jerusalem, so you must also bear witness at Rome."* This word of encouragement came at a challenging time, bolstering Paul's resolve to continue his mission.

Similarly, in Acts 11:23-24, Barnabas, known as the *"son of encouragement,"* visited the church in Antioch and *"encouraged them all that with purpose of heart they should continue with the Lord."* His presence and words provided vital support and encouragement to the believers there.

2. Exhortation

Exhortation through prophecy urges believers to live in accordance with God's will and to uphold higher standards of faith. The letters to the seven churches in Revelation are a prime example of this. Jesus addresses the churches with messages that challenge them to repent, stay faithful, and overcome their struggles. For instance, He advises the church in Ephesus: *"Remember therefore from where you have fallen; repent and do the first works"* (Revelation 2:5).

In Acts 15:32, Judas and Silas, who were also prophets, *"exhorted and strengthened the brethren with many words."* Their prophetic messages were crucial in encouraging early Christians to remain steadfast in their faith.

3. Comfort

Prophecy provides comfort by offering solace and reassurance, especially during tough times. In Isaiah 40:1-2, the prophet delivers a comforting message to Israel: *"Comfort, yes, comfort My people! says your God. Speak comfort to Jerusalem, and cry out to her, that her warfare is ended, that her iniquity is pardoned."* This prophecy was meant to assure the Israelites of God's ongoing love and forgiveness.

Another example is found in 1 Thessalonians 4:13-18, where Paul offers comfort to believers about the resurrection and the second coming of Christ. He concludes with, *"Therefore comfort one another with these words"* (1 Thessalonians 4:18). This prophecy provided hope and reassurance to the early church regarding their future with Christ.

Prophecy and Church Leadership

"This charge I commit to you, son Timothy, according to the prophecies previously made concerning you, that by them you may wage the good warfare."

1 Timothy 1:18

"Do not neglect the gift that is in you, which was given to you by prophecy with the laying on of the hands of the eldership."

1 Timothy 4:14

Apostle Paul addressed Timothy, his young protégé, and emphasised the importance of the prophetic words spoken over him. He charged Timothy to remember and act upon these prophecies as he undertook his ministry. The *"good warfare"* refers to the spiritual battle that Timothy is engaged in as he leads and ministers in the church. Paul's encouragement is rooted in the understanding that prophecies provide divine guidance and strength. By holding onto these prophetic words, Timothy can remain focused and resilient in his mission. The prophecies serve as both a source of inspiration and a reminder of his calling, helping him navigate the challenges and adversities of ministry.

In 1 Timothy 4:14, Paul advises Timothy not to neglect the spiritual gift he has received. This gift was imparted through prophecy and the laying on of hands by the elders. The combination of prophecy and the ceremonial laying on of hands signifies a formal recognition and empowerment of Timothy's gifts and calling. Paul's instruction points out the importance of recognising and nurturing the spiritual gifts that come through prophetic words. These gifts are meant to be actively used in service to the church and in fulfilling God's purposes. By not neglecting these gifts, Timothy is expected to fully embrace his role and responsibilities, using his gifts to edify the church and advance God's work.

Prophecy holds a significant role in guiding and supporting church leadership. It offers divine insight that can shape decisions, provide encouragement, and affirm the direction of leaders and their ministries. Let us examine how prophetic words impact church leadership, focusing on guidance, confirmation, and encouragement.

1. Guidance

Prophecy provides critical guidance to church leaders, helping the leaders navigate complex decisions and discern God's will for their ministries. In the early church, prophetic guidance was instrumental in shaping the direction of ministry efforts. For instance, in Acts 13:2-3, we see the Holy Spirit guiding the early church leaders: *"As they ministered to the Lord and fasted, the Holy Spirit said, 'Now separate to Me Barnabas and Saul for the work to which I have called them.' Then, having fasted and prayed, and laid hands on them, they sent them away."* This prophetic instruction led to the commissioning of Paul and Barnabas for their missionary journeys, demonstrating how prophecy can direct the church's mission and outreach efforts.

Prophetic words help leaders discern the vision and direction for their ministries, aligning their actions with God's broader plan. For instance, prophetic revelations in the Old Testament often guided kings and prophets in making strategic decisions.

2. Confirmation

Prophecy often serves as a confirmation of what church leaders have sensed or been planning. This confirmation reinforces their decisions and validates their course of action. For example, in Acts 21:10-14, the prophet Agabus foretells Paul's imprisonment: *"And as we stayed many days, a certain prophet named Agabus came down from Judea. When he had come to us, he took Paul's belt, bound his own hands and feet, and said, 'Thus says the Holy Spirit, "So shall the Jews at Jerusalem bind the man who owns this belt, and deliver him into the hands of the Gentiles."* The prophecy of Agabus (Acts 21:10-14) served both as a warning and confirmation for Paul, highlighting how prophetic words can prepare and support leaders in their journey. Paul's acceptance of this prophecy reaffirmed his commitment to his calling, despite the impending trials. The prophecy confirmed his understanding of his mission and the sacrifices required.

Prophecies can confirm the callings of individuals within the church, validating their roles and ministries. This affirmation can be crucial for leaders to step confidently into their roles and responsibilities.

3. Encouragement

Prophetic words provide significant encouragement to church leaders, especially during challenging times. They offer reassurance and build confidence, motivating leaders to continue their work with renewed zeal. For instance, in 1 Timothy 1:18, Paul reminds Timothy: *"This charge I commit to you, son Timothy, according to the prophecies previously made concerning you, that by them you may wage the good warfare."* This encouragement through prophecy reminds Timothy of his divine calling and equips him with the assurance needed to face the difficulties of ministry. In Exodus 7:1, God tells Moses, *"See, I have made you as God to Pharaoh, and Aaron your brother shall be your prophet."* This relationship between Moses and Aaron illustrates how prophetic roles can support and complement leadership in guiding the Israelites.

Encouragement through prophecy strengthens leaders' faith and resilience, enabling them to persevere through trials and opposition. This spiritual fortitude is essential for effective leadership and ministry.

What to do with prophecy

We have explored the roles of prophets, the nature of prophecies, and the act of prophesying. Many people eagerly seek to hear what God is saying about their future, especially from a prophet of God. This yearning is not about lacking faith but about the desire to receive divine insight into what lies ahead.

While it is not advisable to constantly search for a prophet and for prophetic words, it is essential to know how to respond when we do receive one. To honour God and benefit from the prophecy, we must take specific steps to ensure its fulfilment. So, what should you do next when a prophetic word is spoken over you?

Chapter Three

What To Do With a Prophetic Word

Receiving a prophetic word can be a profound and life-changing experience. It carries with it the potential to shape your future and direct your steps. However, the moment you receive a prophecy is not the end of the journey; rather, it is the beginning of your active cooperation with God's plan. This chapter will guide you through the essential steps to take when a prophetic word is spoken over you, ensuring that you respond in a way that aligns with Scripture and maximises the potential for fulfilment.

Thank God for the Prophetic Words

"In everything give thanks; for this is the will of God in Christ Jesus for you."

1 Thessalonians 5:18

In the Christian journey, giving thanks is not just a response to positive circumstances but a divine mandate that encompasses all aspects of our lives, including hearing from God. The apostle Paul's instruction to give thanks in everything underscores a profound spiritual principle: gratitude aligns us with God's will and fosters a heart of humility and receptiveness.

When God speaks to us, whether through Scripture, prophetic messages, or the quiet prompting of the Holy Spirit, it is a profound privilege and a testament to His intimate involvement in our lives. Recognising this, we should respond with heartfelt gratitude, acknowledging the grace and mercy that allows us to hear His voice.

Throughout the Bible, we see numerous examples of individuals who thanked God for His guidance and communication:

In the Psalms, David often expresses his gratitude to God for His guidance and provision, even in times of distress. Psalm 28:7 says, *"The Lord is my strength and my shield; my heart trusted in Him, and I am helped; therefore, my heart greatly rejoices, and with my song I will praise Him."* When God revealed Nebuchadnezzar's dream to Daniel, he responded with a prayer of thanksgiving. Daniel 2:23 states, *"I thank You and praise You, O God of my fathers; You have given me wisdom and might and have now made known to me what we asked of You."* The apostle Paul himself consistently models gratitude. In his letters, he frequently thanks God for His guidance and for the faith of other believers, demonstrating an ongoing attitude of thankfulness.

Write It Down

"I will stand my watch and set myself on the rampart and watch to see what He will say to me, and what I will answer when I am corrected. Then the Lord answered me and said: 'Write the vision and make it plain on tablets, that he may run who reads it. For the vision is yet for an appointed time; but at the end it will speak, and it will not lie. Though it tarries, wait for it; because it will surely come, it will not tarry."

Habakkuk 2:1-3

Habakkuk was in deep conversation with God, seeking understanding about the troubling times his nation was going through. Habakkuk intentionally positioned himself to hear from God, and God responded with clear instructions that resonated with timeless significance: *"Write the vision and make it plain on tablets."*

This practice of writing down divine revelations is deeply rooted in biblical tradition. For instance, God commanded Moses to document the Law, ensuring that His commandments were preserved for future generations (Exodus 34:27). Similarly, the prophet Isaiah recorded his visions and prophecies, which continue to guide believers today (Isaiah 30:8). In the New Testament, John is instructed to write down his visions in the book of Revelation, providing a detailed account of prophetic revelations (Revelation 1:19).

Documenting God's messages serves several vital purposes. As Habakkuk 2:1-3 teaches, it ensures clarity, encourages action, and preserves the vision for its appointed time. By maintaining a record of God's communication, we honour His word, facilitate our spiritual growth, and prepare ourselves to witness the fulfilment of His promises. Embracing this discipline aligns us more closely with God's purposes and strengthens our journey of faith.

Test Prophecies

"Beloved, do not believe every spirit, but test the spirits, whether they are of God; because many false prophets have gone out into the world."

1 John 4:1

"Let two or three prophets speak, and let the others judge."

1 Corinthians 14:29

"Test all things; hold fast what is good. Abstain from every form of evil."

1 Thessalonians 5:21-22

In the New Testament, we find clear instructions on how to handle prophecy within the church. These guidelines help us ensure that any prophetic message aligns with God's truth and character.

The Apostle John (1 John 4:1) addresses believers as *"beloved,"* indicating his deep affection and concern for their spiritual wellbeing. In this verse, John warns against the naive acceptance of every spiritual claim or prophetic message. Instead, he instructs believers to *"test the spirits"* to determine their divine origin. This caution arises from the reality that *"many false prophets have gone out into the world."* These false prophets present a danger by promoting deceptive teachings that can lead believers astray. Therefore, discerning the authenticity of spiritual messages is essential for maintaining doctrinal purity and spiritual health within the church, emphasising the need for careful discernment to avoid being misled.

Similarly, 1 Corinthians 14:29 implies that while it is important to allow prophets to share their messages, it is equally important for others in the church to evaluate and discern these messages. This collective discernment helps maintain doctrinal integrity and protects the church from deception.

In his letter to the Thessalonians, Paul provides practical advice for spiritual discernment and moral conduct. He encourages believers to *"test all things,"* implying a thorough examination of teachings, prophecies, and actions to ascertain their truthfulness and alignment with God's will. The phrase *"hold fast what is good"* suggests that, upon testing, believers should cling to what is genuinely beneficial and godly. Conversely, *"abstain from every form of evil"* serves as a warning to avoid anything that deviates from God's standards, reinforcing the need for vigilance and discernment in all aspects of life.

9 Ways to Test a Prophetic Word

When you receive a prophetic word, it is essential to evaluate it carefully. Here are nine tests, grounded in Scripture, to help you discern the authenticity and purpose of the prophecy:

1. Is it Edifying?

Does the prophecy encourage and build you up? According to 1 Corinthians 14:3, *"But he who prophesies speaks edification and exhortation and comfort to men."*

2. Does it Agree with God's Word?

A true prophecy will always align with Scripture. Amos 3:3 says, *"Can two walk together, unless they are agreed?"* Additionally, 2 Peter 1:21 states, *"For prophecy never came by the will of man, but holy men of God spoke as they were moved by the Holy Spirit."*

3. Does it Agree with the Holy Spirit's Character and Nature?

A prophecy should reflect the fruits of the Spirit. Romans 14:7 reminds us, *"For none of us lives to himself, and no one dies to himself."* Galatians 5:22-23 lists the fruits: *"But the fruit of the Spirit is love, joy, peace, longsuffering, kindness, goodness, faithfulness, gentleness, self-control. Against such there is no law."*

4. Does it Come True Over Time?

A genuine prophecy will be fulfilled. Deuteronomy 18:22 teaches, "When a prophet speaks in the name of the Lord, if the thing does not happen or come to pass, that is the thing which the Lord has not spoken; the prophet has spoken it presumptuously; you shall not be afraid of him."

5. Does it Promote Obedience or Disobedience to God?

A prophecy should lead to greater submission to the Holy Spirit. Deuteronomy 13:1-3 warns against prophecies that encourage following other gods, even if the sign or wonder comes to pass.

6. Does it Produce Liberty or Bondage?

True prophecy brings freedom, not fear. Romans 8:15 states, "For you did not receive the spirit of bondage again to fear, but you received the Spirit of adoption by whom we cry out, 'Abba, Father." Also, 2 Corinthians 3:17 says, "Now the Lord is the Spirit; and where the Spirit of the Lord is, there is liberty."

7. Does it Bring Life to the Service?

The prophecy should enliven the congregation. 2 Corinthians 3:6 explains, *"Who also made us sufficient as ministers of the new covenant, not of the letter but of the Spirit; for the letter kills, but the Spirit gives life."*

8. Does it Resonate with Your Spirit?

A prophecy should bear witness with your spirit. 1 John 5:6b states, "And it is the Spirit who bears witness, because the Spirit is truth."

9. Does it Ultimately Give Glory to God?

The final test is whether the prophecy glorifies God. Deuteronomy 13:1-3 again cautions against any prophecy that leads people away from God, underscoring the need for it to align with God's will and bring glory to Him.

By applying these nine tests, you can discern the validity of a prophecy and ensure it aligns with God's Word, the Holy Spirit's nature, and ultimately glorifies God.

Chapter Four

From Prophecy to Reality

The journey from receiving a prophecy to seeing its fulfilment involves thoughtful action and faith. This chapter explores the process of turning prophetic words into reality. By praying with the Holy Spirit, confession - speaking God's promises, staying vigilant and patient, positioning yourself for fulfilment, living out God's promises, and avoiding pitfalls, you can actively participate in the incredible journey of seeing God's word come to life in your own experience.

Praying Through Prophecy with the Holy Spirit

When navigating prophecy, it is crucial to maintain a posture of prayer, supported by the guidance of the Holy Spirit, as we await its fulfilment. Prophecy is a powerful tool, but it is through prayer that we fully engage with and understand its implications.

1 Corinthians 13:9 reminds us, *"For we know in part, and we prophesy in part."* This verse underscores that prophecy provides partial insights, which means we need the Holy Spirit's help to grasp the complete picture and to navigate the path to fulfilment.

In 1 Thessalonians 5:17, Paul instructs us to *"pray without ceasing."* This ongoing prayer is essential not only for our personal spiritual growth but also for responding to prophetic messages. Persistent prayer keeps us aligned with God's will and opens our hearts to the Spirit's leading. Ephesians 6:18 further emphasises the need for constant prayer: *"Praying always with all prayer and supplication in the Spirit."* This highlights that our prayers should be infused with the Spirit's guidance, ensuring that we are praying in harmony with God's will and staying vigilant as we await the realisation of prophecies.

Romans 8:26 provides assurance that the Holy Spirit assists us in our weaknesses, especially when we struggle to find the right words to pray: *"Likewise the Spirit also helps in our weaknesses; for we do not know what we should pray for as we ought, but the Spirit Himself makes intercession for us with groanings which cannot be uttered."* The Spirit's intercession ensures that our prayers are effective, even when we are uncertain.

Daniel's experience in Daniel 9:3-4 exemplifies this approach. He earnestly sought God through prayer, fasting, and supplication, demonstrating a deep commitment to understanding and awaiting God's guidance. His example teaches us the importance of dedicating ourselves to prayer as we anticipate the fulfilment of prophetic words.

In Daniel 10:1-14, Daniel's extended period of prayer and mourning illustrates the necessity of perseverance. His vision, revealed after much prayer, underscores the value of remaining steadfast and prayerful while waiting for God's promises to unfold.

Simeon, as described in Luke 2:25-35, embodies the spirit of patient expectation through prayer. He awaited the Messiah with prayerful anticipation and was rewarded with the sight of Jesus, demonstrating how fervent prayer prepares us to recognise and embrace God's promises.

Similarly, Anna the prophetess in Luke 2:36-38, dedicated her life to fasting and prayer. Her story highlights how prayerfully engaging with God's promises enables us to be in tune with His timing and purposes.

Through prayer and guidance from the Holy Spirit, we can effectively navigate the time between receiving a prophecy and seeing it fulfilled. Constant prayer keeps us closely connected to God, helps us remain attuned to the Spirit's direction, and prepares our hearts to experience the fulfilment of His promises.

Confess It and Speak It Out

In John 6:63, Jesus says, *"It is the Spirit who gives life; the flesh profits nothing. The words that I speak to you are spirit, and they are life."* This highlights the profound power of our words; once spoken, they can shape our reality in ways that align with God's will.

To see a prophecy come to fruition, it is essential to speak it out with faith. For example, in Luke 1:11-17, we see the angel Gabriel delivering a prophecy to Zechariah about the birth of John the Baptist. For this prophecy to be realised, Zechariah's scepticism is addressed in Luke 1:15-20, where the angel draws attention to the importance of believing and speaking in accordance with God's message.

Jesus reinforces this principle in Mark 11:12-14, where He answers the barren fig tree, demonstrating the impact of speaking words of faith and authority. Later, in Mark 11:20-24, He teaches about the power of speaking in faith, encouraging believers to pray and speak with conviction. Similarly, Proverbs 18:21 tells us, *"Death and life are in the power of the tongue,"* underscoring the importance of our words.

Luke 6:45 reminds us that our words reflect what is in our hearts, while Romans 10:8-10 explains how confession with our mouth and belief in our heart are essential for salvation. In Genesis 17:1-5 and 15-16,21, we see God changing Abram's name to Abraham as a declaration of his future role as the father of many nations, showing how God's promises are tied to spoken declarations.

Hebrews 10:23 encourages us to hold fast to our confession of hope without wavering, reflecting the importance of consistent and faithful speech. Romans 4:21 shows Abraham's unwavering faith in God's promises, which he spoke and believed. Ephesians 5:1 urges us to be imitators of God, reflecting His nature in our words and actions, while Deuteronomy 8:3 reminds us that man does not live by bread alone but by every word that proceeds from the mouth of the Lord, highlighting the life-giving power of God's words.

In essence, speaking out and confessing the promises and prophecies you receive is not just about vocalising them; it is about aligning your heart and actions with God's will, trusting that His words will indeed come to pass.

Be Watchful, Patient, and Expectant

Revelation 3:2 commands us to *"Be watchful, and strengthen the things which remain, that are ready to die: for I have not found your works perfect before God."* This calls us to be vigilant in our spiritual journey, ensuring that we are always alert and ready to fortify our faith.

Nehemiah 4:9 provides a powerful example of this vigilance: *"Nevertheless, we made our prayer to our God, and because of them we set a watch against them day and night."* Being watchful means being constantly on guard, in prayer, and attentive to our surroundings. Psalm 141:3 reinforces the importance of being cautious with our words: *"Set a guard, O Lord, over my mouth; keep watch over the door of my lips."*

In Matthew 26:40-41, Jesus rebukes His disciples for failing to stay awake and pray: *"Then He came to the disciples and found them sleeping, and said to Peter, 'What! Could you not watch with Me one hour? Watch and pray, lest you enter temptation. The spirit indeed is willing, but the flesh is weak."* This highlights the necessity of staying vigilant and prayerful.

Paul urges us in 1 Corinthians 16:13 to *"Watch, stand fast in the faith, be brave, be strong."* Similarly, in 2 Timothy 4:5, he advises, *"But you be watchful in all things, endure afflictions, do the work of an evangelist, fulfil your ministry."* This underscores the importance of constant vigilance in all aspects of our spiritual lives.

Luke 12:37 assures us of the blessings of watchfulness: *"Blessed are those servants whom the master, when he comes, will find watching. Assuredly, I say to you that he will gird himself and have them sit down to eat and will come and serve them."* Ephesians 6:18 further encourages us to be persistent in prayer and watchfulness: *"Praying always with all prayer and supplication in the Spirit, being watchful to this end with all perseverance and supplication for all the saints."* Paul's personal experiences of vigilance in 2 Corinthians 6:5 and 11:27 highlight the trials and hardships that come with being constantly watchful.

Equally important is patience and expectation. Luke 8:15 describes the good ground as those who *"having heard the word with a noble and good heart, keep it and bear fruit with patience."* Patience is crucial in seeing the fulfilment of God's promises. Psalm 62:5 encourages us to wait expectantly: *"My soul, wait silently for God alone, for my expectation is from Him."*

Proverbs 23:18 promises a hopeful future: *"For surely there is a hereafter, and your hope will not be cut off."* Similarly, Proverbs 24:14 reassures us of the reward for wisdom: *"So shall the knowledge of wisdom be to your soul; if you have found it, there is a prospect, and your hope will not be cut off."*

The parable of the ten virgins in Matthew 25:1-13 illustrates the importance of being prepared and patient, waiting expectantly for the bridegroom. Hebrews 10:35-38 urges us not to lose confidence: *"Therefore do not cast away your confidence, which has great reward. For you have need of endurance, so that after you have done the will of God, you may receive the promise."*

These qualities prepare us to receive and fulfil God's prophecies and promises in our lives, aligning us with His timing and purposes, and setting our hearts and minds for the realisation of His divine will.

Position Yourself for the Fulfilment of Prophecy

Align your life with God's requirements. For example, Revelation 2:7 says, *"He who has an ear, let him hear what the Spirit says to the churches."* This means being attentive to God's voice and open to His guidance. Additionally, 2 Timothy 2:3-6 encourages enduring hardship and following the rules, like a soldier or athlete, to receive God's promises. Living a life of obedience, faithfulness, and perseverance sets the foundation for receiving His promises.

Actively nurture and develop the gifts God has given you. 2 Timothy 1:6 reminds us to fan into flame the spiritual gift within us. This could involve studying the Bible more diligently, engaging in regular prayer, or using your talents to serve others. By actively engaging with and using our spiritual gifts, we keep our faith vibrant and position ourselves to fulfil God's purposes.

Keep the prophecy in mind and take proactive steps toward its fulfilment. In John 20:18, Jesus spoke to Peter about his future, encouraging him to prepare. Similarly, 2 Peter 1:14 and Acts 12:1-6 illustrate how understanding and anticipation shape our actions. Constantly reflecting on God's words and working towards their realisation show our faith. This might include setting specific goals related to your prophecy or seeking guidance from spiritual mentors.

Follow His specific directives, such as waiting in Jerusalem for the Holy Spirit as instructed in Luke 24:49, Acts 1:4-8, and

Acts 2:1-4. Jesus' disciples were told to stay in Jerusalem until they received the Holy Spirit, which empowered them for their mission. Obedience and patience are essential in positioning ourselves to receive God's promises.

Maintain regular church attendance, worship, and a growing love for God, as emphasised in Hebrews 10:24-25. Being part of a faith community and regularly worshipping God strengthens our faith and keeps us aligned with His purposes. This involves participating in church activities, Bible studies, and fellowship groups, which can provide encouragement and accountability.

Demonstrate your faith through tangible actions. Luke 1:44 shows the response to faith, and Isaiah 55:10-11 highlights the certainty of God's word. Faith is made evident through our actions, as we step out and live according to God's promises. Acting on your faith could involve making decisions that reflect your trust in God's promises, such as pursuing a new opportunity or offering help to someone in need.

Trust wholeheartedly in the fulfilment of God's promises. Luke 1:45 speaks of the blessing for those who believe, and Hebrews 11:1, 6 reinforces the essence of faith. Trusting God's word means having confidence that what He has spoken will come to pass, even if we do not see it immediately. This belief fuels our actions and keeps us aligned with His plans.

Living Out God's Promises

In Genesis 26:1-5, Isaac faced a severe famine, but he chose to invest in his future by continuing to cultivate the land. This act of faith and diligence resulted in a bountiful harvest. Similarly, when God's promises seem distant, focus on personal growth and preparation. Strengthen your skills, deepen your understanding of Scripture, and build your character. This proactive approach not only prepares you for the fulfilment of God's promises but also aligns you with His purpose.

Isaac's decision to sow crops during a famine (Genesis 26:12-13) exemplifies the power of faith-driven action. Despite the difficult circumstances, he acted on the promise of God's provision and saw a hundredfold return. Your actions, motivated by faith, can unlock God's blessings. It is essential to move forward with confidence and take practical steps that align with the vision God has given you.

Zechariah and Elizabeth's story (Luke 1:7, 23-24) demonstrates the importance of acting upon God's promises. Despite their advanced age, they embraced God's promise of a child and took the necessary steps to make it a reality. Their actions - returning home to be together - show us that faith involves more than waiting; it requires taking deliberate actions in response to God's promises.

The story of Sarah's initial scepticism (Genesis 18:14-15) and eventual belief in God's promise illustrates how faith must be unwavering. James 2:14-17 emphasises that faith without action is dead. Trust in God's promises should not be undermined by doubt. Align your actions with your faith, even when the fulfilment seems far off.

Mary's response to the angel (Luke 1:38) highlights how we should adapt our lives in accordance with God's word. Her willingness to embrace her role in the fulfilment of God's promise demonstrates the need for readiness to adjust our lives and make sacrifices in alignment with His plan.

Joseph's acceptance of God's plan, despite potential ridicule (Matthew 1:18-25), underscores the necessity of obedience. His willingness to marry Mary, even though it exposed him to public scrutiny, shows that cooperating with God's plan often requires courage and a willingness to face challenges.

Ecclesiastes 5:4-5 and Deuteronomy 23:21, 23 stress the importance of fulfilling the promises you make to God. Hannah's story (1 Samuel 1:11, 26-28) serves as a powerful example. She honoured her vow to dedicate her son Samuel to God, and in return, she received more than she had initially asked for. Keeping your commitments strengthens your relationship with God and aligns you with His promises.

Manoah's act of offering a sacrifice after receiving a prophecy (Judges 13:2, 15-23) demonstrates the significance of sowing seeds of faith. His willingness to give thanks and make offerings in response to God's message paved the way for the fulfilment of the prophecy about his son Samson. Investing in faith through acts of worship and gratitude helps to set the stage for God's promises to come to fruition.

To see God's promises fulfilled, it is crucial to develop yourself, take decisive action, maintain unwavering faith, adapt your life according to God's word, and sow seeds of faith. These practices ensure that you are not only aligned with God's purpose but also actively participating in the realisation of His promises. Through these steps, you prepare yourself to experience the blessings and fulfilment of God's divine plans.

Avoid Undermining God's Promises

Impatience can lead us to seek shortcuts that undermine God's promises. In Genesis 16, Sarah's impatience led to her decision to have Abraham father a child with Hagar, which resulted in complications and conflict. Similarly, rushing ahead of God's timing or taking matters into our own hands can jeopardise the fulfilment of His promises. It is crucial to wait on God's timing and avoid making decisions driven by impatience or frustration.

Divine timing is essential to the fulfilment of God's promises. Acts 10:9-19 recounts how Peter's vision and subsequent visit to Cornelius were perfectly timed by God. The timing of the vision was crucial for the spread of the Gospel to the Gentiles. Understanding and aligning with God's divine timing requires patience and trust. Avoid forcing your own agenda and instead seek to recognise and follow God's timing in every situation.

Sin and disobedience can derail the fulfilment of God's promises. Consider the 'Eli factor' from 1 Samuel 2:30, where Eli's failure to discipline his sons resulted in God's judgment on his house. Similarly, the 'Saul factor' (1 Samuel 15:26-28) shows how King Saul's disobedience to God's command led to his rejection as king. Maintaining a righteous life and adhering to God's commands are vital to ensuring that we do not undermine the promises He has made to us.

Obedience to God's instructions is crucial for seeing His promises fulfilled. Isaiah 48:18 highlights the blessings that come from following God's commands closely. God's instructions are meant to guide us towards the fulfilment of His promises and plans for our lives. Ignoring or deviating from these instructions can hinder the realisation of what He has promised.

Self-prophecy, or speaking God's promises into our own lives, can be a powerful tool. Isaiah 3:10 encourages us to proclaim God's promises for our lives, while John 4:35-36 speaks about the joy and reward of seeing God's promises fulfilled. Speaking positively and aligning our words with God's promises helps to reinforce our faith and expectation.

Patience, careful adherence to instructions, and righteous living are essential to witnessing the full and fruitful realisation of God's promises.

Chapter Five

The Fruit of Prophecy

Throughout this chapter, I emphasise a human-centred approach to prophecy - one that calls for active involvement, careful discernment, and a readiness to respond. By fully embracing the fruit of prophecy, believers can experience significant spiritual growth, contribute to positive community transformation, and witness the fulfilment of God's promises in their lives.

Spiritual Growth and Maturity

Prophecy plays a significant role in fostering spiritual growth and maturity, guiding believers towards a deeper understanding of God's will and a more profound relationship with Him. More importantly, prophecy contributes to spiritual development and the pursuit of growing in the knowledge and grace of Jesus Christ, as well as promoting unity in the faith.

Prophecy provides specific guidance and direction

from God, offering insights into His plans and purposes. This divine guidance helps believers make decisions that align with God's will, fostering spiritual growth as they learn to follow His direction. Proverbs 29:18 says, *"Where there is no revelation, the people cast off restraint; but happy is he who keeps the law."*

Prophetic messages can also encourage, correct, and refine believers. They bring comfort and challenge, leading to personal transformation and deeper alignment with God's purposes. Revelation 19:10 highlights that *"the testimony of Jesus is the spirit of prophecy,"* underscoring that prophecy reveals and confirms Christ's ongoing work in our lives.

Prophecy often reveals deeper truths about Jesus Christ, enhancing our understanding of His nature, character, and the scope of His work. This revelation helps believers grasp the significance of Christ's role in their lives and the world. John 16:13-14 illustrates this: *"When He, the Spirit of truth, has come, He will guide you into all truth… He will glorify Me, for He will take of what is Mine and declare it to you."*

Through prophecy, believers receive direct messages from God that can draw them closer to Christ. These messages often highlight aspects of Jesus' grace, love, and power, encouraging believers to deepen their relationship with Him. Ephesians 3:16-17 prays for believers to be *"strengthened with might through His Spirit in the inner man, that Christ may dwell in your hearts through faith."*

Prophetic messages can highlight areas where believers need to grow in grace, urging them to develop Christlike qualities. As believers heed these messages, they learn to embody the fruits of the Spirit and live out their faith more authentically. 2 Peter 3:18 encourages us to *"grow in the grace and knowledge of our Lord and Saviour Jesus Christ."*

Prophecy helps believers build character and resilience. The process of receiving, interpreting, and acting on prophetic messages cultivates spiritual maturity and strengthens faith. Romans 5:3-4 teaches that *"tribulation produces perseverance; and perseverance, character; and character, hope."*

Prophecy serves to unite believers by focusing them on common goals and divine purposes. When prophecy is shared within a community, it can bring a sense of collective direction and purpose, fostering unity and collaboration. Ephesians 4:11-13 highlights the goal of spiritual gifts, including prophecy, to *"equip the saints for the work of ministry, for the edifying of the body of Christ... till we all come to the unity of the faith and of the knowledge of the Son of God."*

Prophecy encourages believers to support one another and work together towards spiritual growth. It fosters an environment where believers are actively involved in each other's lives, building a strong, united community of faith. 1 Corinthians 14:26 underscores this by stating, "Let all things be done for edification," ensuring that prophetic messages contribute to the overall growth and unity of the church.

The ultimate goal of spiritual growth and maturity is to become more like Christ. Prophecy contributes to this goal by revealing aspects of Christ's character and will, guiding believers in their journey towards Christlikeness. Colossians 1:10-11 encourages believers to "walk worthy of the Lord, fully pleasing Him, being fruitful in every good work and increasing in the knowledge of God."

Prophecy strengthens believers' faith by providing confirmation of God's promises and encouraging them to trust in His plans. It helps believers remain steadfast in their faith journey, even in challenging times. Hebrews 10:23 encourages us to "hold fast the confession of our hope without wavering, for He who promised is faithful."

Prophecy and Community Impact

Prophetic ministry has been pivotal in guiding and shaping communities throughout church history, significantly impacting how believers are mobilised for missions, acts of service, and collective actions. Here are some key examples of how prophetic words have influenced communities and guided collective efforts, with relevant Bible references:

In Acts 13:1-3, the church in Antioch was engaged in worship and fasting when the Holy Spirit spoke through a prophetic message: *"Now separate to Me Barnabas and Saul for the work to which I have called them."* This prophecy led to the commissioning of Paul and Barnabas for their first missionary journey. The response of the Antioch church to this prophecy was crucial for the expansion of the early church and the spread of the Gospel.

Acts 15 recounts a significant theological dispute regarding the inclusion of Gentiles in the church. Prophetic guidance, along with the leadership of James, was instrumental in reaching a consensus. James referenced the prophecy of Amos (Amos 9:11-12) to support the decision that Gentiles should not be burdened with the full yoke of Jewish law. This prophetic insight facilitated a unified approach to their inclusion in the faith.

William Carey, known as the father of modern missions, was deeply influenced by prophetic encouragement. His vision for global missions, confirmed by prophetic words, led him to pioneer work in India. Carey's efforts, guided by prophetic insight, established missions and churches across India, leaving a lasting impact on global Christianity.

The early 20th-century Azusa Street Revival in Los Angeles, led by William Seymour, was marked by prophetic experiences and revelations. This revival played a key role in the birth of the Pentecostal movement. Prophetic words and visions during this time inspired believers to engage in acts of service and missions, fostering racial and social reconciliation and contributing to the global spread of Pentecostalism (Acts 2:4).

In contemporary settings, prophetic words have mobilised churches to tackle social issues and engage in acts of service. For example, prophetic messages have inspired churches to initiate ministries for the homeless, combat human trafficking, and support orphanages (Matthew 25:35-40). These actions reflect God's heart for justice and compassion.

Prophetic ministry has often sparked and sustained revival movements throughout history. The Welsh Revival of 1904-1905, for instance, was characterised by prophetic messages and visions leading to widespread repentance and renewed commitment to prayer and service. This revival resulted in significant social changes and community transformation, including increased involvement in social justice and charity (2 Chronicles 7:14).

Today, prophetic ministry continues to guide global missions' efforts. Churches and mission organisations seek prophetic insight to identify regions and people groups in need of outreach (Matthew 28:19). Prophetic words have directed mission efforts to unreached areas or regions experiencing crises.

Prophetic ministry often inspires and directs church planting and social justice initiatives. For example, prophetic words have led churches to establish congregations in underserved areas or address systemic issues such as racial inequality and environmental degradation (Isaiah 58:6-7).

Prophetic ministry has been instrumental in guiding communities and mobilising collective actions throughout history. It provides divine guidance and direction, aligning the church's efforts with God's purposes and inspiring believers to engage in missions, acts of service, and community impact. The role of prophecy in these efforts highlights the importance of staying attuned to the Holy Spirit's leading to fulfil God's call to action.

Testimonies of Prophetic Fulfilment

There is an old saying that 'prophecy does not fall into your lap.' This means that when you receive a prophetic word or message, in most cases, you cannot simply 'go home and sleep,' expecting it to come true on its own. Instead, you need to respond with actions that demonstrate your faith and anticipation of the prophecy's fulfilment. The Bible provides numerous examples of individuals who received prophetic words and took significant faith actions in response. Anna praying until fulfilment (Luke 2:36-38), Noah building the ark (Genesis 6:13-22) and Abraham acting on God's promise (Genesis 17:1-5, 15-16, 21).

Sharing testimonies of individuals who have experienced the fulfilment of prophetic words can be deeply encouraging. The testimonies of biblical figures like Anna, Noah, and Abraham, along with modern examples demonstrate that prophecy requires active participation. When we receive a prophetic word, it is our responsibility to take faith-driven actions that align with and show our expectation for its fulfilment. These actions, coupled with unwavering faith, enable us to witness the realisation of God's promises in our lives. Sharing such testimonies encourages and inspires others to embrace prophecy with humility, faith, and discernment, walking closely with God to fulfil His divine purposes.

In this section, I will share some testimonies and present analysis of each one to highlight the various faith-driven actions taken in expectation of the prophecy's realisation.

Testimony of Joan and Her Business

Joan, a small business owner, was at a church service when she received a prophetic word about her business facing financial difficulties. The prophecy, shared by a trusted minister, predicted a season of growth and success despite the current challenges. Joan was encouraged to take practical steps, like refining her business strategy and increasing her outreach efforts.

Though the initial period was tough, Joan prayerfully and faithfully applied the guidance from the prophecy. Over the next year, her business not only recovered but thrived, exceeding her expectations. This experience strengthened her faith and confirmed the truth of the prophetic word in her life, showing how prophecy can provide direction and reassurance during uncertain times.

Lessons from Joan's Testimony

Joan received the prophecy from a trusted minister, which helped her accept the message with an open heart. She believed in the prophetic word, trusting it as a message from God about her business. This faith was crucial and set the stage for her subsequent actions. Joan made concrete changes to improve her business strategy, which likely included, analysing market trends and consumer behaviour to better align her products or services with demand, reviewing her financial practices to manage resources more effectively during tough times, and streamlining operations to reduce costs and improve productivity.

Despite facing financial difficulties, Joan remained consistent in applying the guidance from the prophecy. She did not give up but continued to work diligently on her business. Her ability to withstand the initial struggles without losing hope was a testament to her resilience. She trusted that the difficult period was temporary and part of the prophetic promise.

Over the next year, Joan's business not only recovered but thrived beyond her expectations. The fulfilment of the prophecy strengthened her faith, confirming that the prophetic word was true, and God was faithful to His promise. The experience served as a personal testimony of how prophecy can provide direction and reassurance in uncertain times.

Testimony of Sarah and Her Healing

Sarah, who had been struggling with a long-term health issue, received a prophetic word about healing during a church service. The prophecy spoke of restoration and health, which deeply encouraged her and gave her hope.

Sarah continued to pray and trust in the prophecy while pursuing medical treatment. Over time, her condition improved significantly, and she experienced a level of recovery that her doctors had not anticipated. This fulfilment of the prophetic word not only strengthened her faith but also confirmed her belief in God's healing power and timing.

Lessons from Sarah's Testimony

Sarah accepted the prophetic word with faith. The word gave her hope and strengthened her belief in the possibility of healing. She maintained her trust in God's promise of restoration, reflecting a heart full of faith.

Sarah continued to pray fervently, seeking God's healing. This persistent prayer was an act of faith, demonstrating her reliance on God and His promises. Through prayer, Sarah kept her focus on God, aligning her heart and mind with His will.

Despite her belief in the prophecy, Sarah did not neglect the practical step of seeking medical treatment. She continued her medical appointments and followed the prescribed treatments.

By pursuing medical treatment, Sarah showed that she combined faith with practical action, demonstrating wisdom in her approach to healing.

The prophetic word instilled a sense of hope and positivity in Sarah, which likely contributed to her overall wellbeing and aided her recovery. She lived with the expectation that the prophecy would come true, which influenced her outlook and actions positively.

Testimony of David and His Family

David and his family were facing significant financial difficulties and emotional strain. During a church service, they received a prophetic word about a breakthrough in their circumstances and a promise of peace and provision.

In response to the prophecy, David took practical steps, such as seeking financial advice and finding ways to support his family emotionally. Gradually, their financial situation improved, and they experienced an unexpected provision that aligned with the prophetic word. This testimony encouraged them and reinforced their faith in God's provision and care.

Lessons from David and His Family

David proactively sought financial advice to better manage their resources and find solutions to their financial problems. Consulting financial advisors or seeking counsel from knowledgeable individuals helped David gain insight into effective financial management and strategies for improving their economic situation.

David focused on providing emotional support to his family, ensuring that they remained united and strong during the challenging period. This involved regular family discussions, fostering open communication, and possibly seeking professional counselling to address any emotional or psychological issues within the family.

The family likely increased their prayer efforts, seeking God's guidance and intervention in their situation. This might have included daily family prayers, fasting, and participating in church prayer meetings to reinforce their faith and reliance on God's promises.

Despite the difficulties, David maintained a positive attitude, demonstrating his faith in the prophetic word they had received. This positive mindset was crucial in motivating the family to persevere and remain hopeful, even when immediate results were not visible.

David remained vigilant for any opportunities that could help improve their situation. This included being open to new job offers, business opportunities, or any unexpected provision that came their way, aligning with the prophetic word of breakthrough and provision.

Gradually, their financial situation began to improve as they implemented the advice received and took advantage of new opportunities. They experienced unexpected provision that aligned with the prophetic word, further validating the prophecy. The family grew closer and more resilient emotionally, supporting each other through the difficult times.

Testimony of James

James, an immigrant from Africa, found himself struggling with significant financial difficulties while trying to balance his academics, tuition fees, and rent payments. He was working a part-time night job that barely covered his needs.

Amidst this challenging period, James recalled a prophetic word he had received before leaving his home country for the UK: "You may not see the wind; you may not see the rain, but the ditches shall be filled with water - you will not be stranded." This message was reaffirmed during a church service he attended in the UK.

Embracing the prophecy, James renewed his prayer efforts, continued serving faithfully in his church, and maintained a positive attitude at work. One day, his manager approached him with an unexpected opportunity. There was an opening for a part-time position in his department, and they wanted James to fill it. Grateful for this new opening, James accepted the offer.

This new job allowed James to work full-time while studying during the day. With the increased income, he was able to pay his tuition fees, cover his rent, and meet his other financial responsibilities. Ultimately, James graduated with a Master's degree and celebrated his achievement, recognising it as an answer to his prayers and a fulfilment of the prophetic word he had received.

Lessons from James' Testimony

James received a prophetic word before leaving his home country, which was reaffirmed during a church service in the UK. The prophecy stated: "You may not see the wind; you may not see the rain, but the ditches shall be filled with water - you will not be stranded."

James recalled this prophecy during a challenging time, providing him with hope and encouragement. He intensified his prayer life, seeking divine guidance and support to navigate his difficult circumstances.

Despite his struggles, James remained committed to serving in his church. This act of faith likely provided him with spiritual strength and community support. He maintained a positive attitude in his part-time night job, which is crucial for fostering good relationships and demonstrating reliability. His positive attitude and diligence at work did not go unnoticed. It is implied that his consistent performance and willingness to go above and beyond contributed to his manager considering him for a new opportunity.

When presented with a new part-time position in his department, James was ready and willing to accept the opportunity. This demonstrates his openness to new avenues that could potentially fulfil the prophetic word. He gratefully accepted the new job offer, recognising it as a potential fulfilment of the prophecy. This step required faith and a proactive attitude towards change.

The new position allowed James to work full-time while continuing his studies during the day. Managing this balance required discipline, time management, and perseverance.

The full-time position provided James with a higher income, enabling him to pay his tuition fees, cover rent, and meet other financial obligations. This financial stability was a direct answer to the specific challenges he was facing.

With his financial burdens alleviated, James could focus better on his academics and personal responsibilities, leading to improved overall wellbeing.

James successfully completed his Master's degree, a significant milestone that marked the culmination of his hard work, faith, and perseverance. James celebrated his graduation as a fulfilment of the prophetic word, acknowledging God's guidance and provision throughout his journey.

Chapter Six

What to do When Prophecies Delay

In this chapter, I will explore what to do when you have received a prophetic word, but its fulfilment seems to be taking longer than expected. This period of waiting can be challenging, filled with uncertainty and the temptation to lose hope. However, understanding how to traverse this time can strengthen your faith and keep you aligned with God's purpose. Before we go further to discuss what to do, I need to share with us what not to do.

5 Things *Not* to Do When Prophecies Delay

Here are a few key things *not* to do when it seems like the fulfilment of a prophecy is delayed.

1. Do not Doubt God's Promise

It is easy to start doubting whether the prophecy was genuine or if God will really come through. Remember that doubt can undermine your faith and disrupt your spiritual growth. James 1:6 warns us, *"But let him ask in faith, with no doubting, for he who doubts is like a wave of the sea driven and tossed by the wind."*

2. Do not Rush Ahead of God's Timing

Resist the urge to take matters into your own hands or force the prophecy to come to pass. This can lead to unnecessary mistakes and frustration. As seen in the story of Abraham and Hagar (Genesis 16), rushing ahead of God's plan can have long-term consequences.

3. Do not Fall into Discouragement

Prolonged waiting can lead to discouragement, but it is crucial not to let it take root. Discouragement can lead to spiritual lethargy and a lack of trust in God. Instead, keep your eyes on God's faithfulness and His past dealings in your life.

4. Do not Compare Your Journey with Others

Avoid comparing your progress or the timing of your fulfilment with that of others. Comparison can lead to envy, frustration, and unnecessary pressure. God's plan for you is unique, and His timing for your life is perfectly tailored to you.

5. Do not Neglect Your Relationship with God

In times of delay, it is easy to become so focused on the promise that you neglect your personal relationship with God. Do not let the waiting period distance you from God. Keep nurturing your relationship through prayer, worship, and Bible study.

7 Truths for Navigating God's Timing

Understanding and accepting God's timing is vital, especially when it feels like the fulfilment of a prophecy is taking longer than we expected. The Bible teaches us that God's timing is different from ours, and recognising this helps us remain patient and trusting when delays occur. Let us explore how to navigate these delays, ensuring that we stay in step with God's perfect plan.

1. Recognise God's Sovereignty Over Time

The first thing we need to do when faced with delays is to acknowledge that God is in control of time. Ecclesiastes 3:1 reminds us, *"To everything there is a season, a time for every purpose under heaven."* This means that God has set specific times for everything in our lives, including the fulfilment of His promises. Our schedules and expectations do not dictate these moments - God's perfect plan does.

Therefore, consciously let go of your own expectations about when things should happen. Pray and consciously tell God that you trust His timing, even when it does not match your own plans. This act of surrender allows you to rest in the assurance that God's timing is better than ours.

Spend time reflecting on bible stories where God's timing differed from human expectations. Think about Joseph, who waited many years after his prophetic dreams before they came true, or David, who was anointed king long before he actually took the throne. These examples remind us that God's timing, although different, is always perfect.

2. Trust the Process God Has in Place

God's timing often involves a process, and this process is just as important as the fulfilment itself. Peter writes, *"With the Lord one day is as a thousand years, and a thousand years as one day"* (2 Peter 3:8), emphasising that God's understanding of time is vastly different from ours. What seems like a delay to us may be an essential part of God's preparation.

Patience is not just about waiting; it is about trusting God during the wait. Rather than getting frustrated or anxious, use this time to develop patience. James 1:4 tells us, *"But let patience have its perfect work, that you may be perfect and complete, lacking nothing."* Pray for patience and for the grace to endure the waiting period.

Understand that this waiting time is an opportunity for personal growth. God might be using this period to prepare you for what is coming. Ask God to show you areas in your life that need refining, and work on them. Whether it's building character, strengthening your faith, or developing new skills, use this time to get ready for the fulfilment of the prophecy.

3. Embrace your Season of Preparation

When God delays the fulfilment of a prophecy, it often means He is preparing you - or the situation around you - for what is to come. Just as a farmer waits for the right season to harvest, we must wait for the right season in our lives for God's promises to be realised. Embracing this season of preparation is crucial.

While you wait, actively prepare yourself for the prophecy's fulfilment. For example, if the prophecy is about a new career, consider taking courses or gaining experience that will help you in that field. Taking steps that align with the prophecy shows your readiness and faith.

Use this season to deepen your relationship with God. Regular prayer, Bible study, and worship will keep you spiritually sharp and aligned with God's will. Staying close to God during this time ensures that you are ready when the fulfilment comes.

4. Stay Encouraged and Guard Against Discouragement

When it feels like the fulfilment of a prophecy is delayed, it is easy to become discouraged. However, it is essential to stay encouraged, knowing that God is faithful, and His promises are true. Discouragement can weaken your faith and distract you from God's plan.

Surround yourself with people who will uplift you and encourage your faith. Connect with a community of believers who can support you with prayer and positive reinforcement. As Hebrews 10:25 advises, do not *"forsake the assembling of ourselves together, as is the manner of some, but exhorting one another."*

Regularly declare God's promises over your life. Speak out Scriptures that affirm His faithfulness, such as Jeremiah 29:11: *"For I know the thoughts that I think toward you, says the Lord, thoughts of peace and not of evil, to give you a future and a hope."* Speaking God's word reinforces your faith and keeps your focus on His promises.

5. Maintain Faith and Expectancy

It is vital to keep your faith strong and wait with expectancy. God's promises will come to pass, but they require us to maintain faith and stay expectant. Waiting expectantly means hoping and believing that God will fulfil His word, even when there is no visible sign yet.

Continually meditate on the Scriptures and the

prophetic word you've received. Keep these words fresh in your mind and heart and let them fuel your faith. Memorise verses that relate to the promises you're waiting for and pray over them regularly.

Thank God for the fulfilment of the prophecy, even before it happens. Praising Him in advance is an act of faith. It shifts your focus from the delay to God's faithfulness and keeps your heart filled with hope.

6. Trust in God's Plan

It is easy to feel discouraged especially when it seems like nothing is happening. During these times, one wonders if God's promises will ever come true, but it is in these very moments that our trust in Him needs to grow stronger.

Take the story of Abraham and Sarah, for example. They waited many long years for God's promise of a son to be fulfilled. Despite the delay, Abraham clung to God's word, and in the end, it happened exactly as God said it would. In Genesis 15:4-5, it says, *"And behold, the word of the Lord came to him, saying, 'This one shall not be your heir, but one who will come from your own body shall be your heir.' Then He brought him outside and said, 'Look now toward heaven, and count the stars if you are able to number them.' And He said to him, 'So shall your descendants be."*

Even though Abraham and Sarah had their moments of doubt and impatience, God's promise was fulfilled as we see in Genesis 21:1-2: *"And the Lord visited Sarah as He had said, and the Lord did for Sarah as He had spoken. For Sarah conceived and bore Abraham a son in his old age, at the set time of which God had spoken to him."*

Their journey reminds us that God's timing is always perfect, even when it feels like it is taking longer than we had hoped. Trusting in God's plan means believing that He is working everything out behind the scenes, even when we cannot see it. It is about having faith that His promises are real and that He will bring them to pass at just the right moment, just as He did for Abraham and Sarah.

7. Resist Impatience

Impatience can often push us into making rash decisions and taking paths that lead us away from God's best for our lives. It is a natural feeling when things are not moving as quickly as we would like, but it is important to resist the urge to take matters into our own hands.

Take the example of King Saul. His impatience ended up costing him his kingdom. Instead of waiting for God's timing, Saul decided to act on his own, offering a sacrifice that only the prophet Samuel was meant to offer. This hasty decision showed a lack of trust in God's timing, and it had serious consequences. As we read in 1 Samuel 13:13-14, Samuel said to Saul, *"You have done foolishly. You have not kept the commandment of the Lord your God, which He commanded you. For now, the Lord would have established your kingdom over Israel forever. But now your kingdom shall not continue. The Lord has sought for Himself a man after His own heart, and the Lord has commanded him to be commander over His people, because you have not kept what the Lord commanded you."*

Saul's story is a powerful reminder that impatience can lead to choices that derail God's plans for us. Waiting on God's timing may be difficult, but it is always the wisest and most rewarding path to take. When we resist impatience, we demonstrate our trust in God, knowing that His timing is perfect and that He is working all things together for our good.

14 Ways to Stay Faithful Whilst You Wait

1. Hold on to Faith

Waiting can be one of the most difficult aspects of our spiritual journey. These periods test and refine our faith, challenging us to trust in God's promises even when there's no immediate sign that they're coming to pass. Hebrews 11:1 reminds us that *"faith is the substance of things hoped for, the evidence of things not seen."* This verse encourages us to keep our faith alive, even when circumstances seem to contradict what God has spoken over our lives.

When you find yourself in a season of waiting, it is essential to take practical steps to maintain and strengthen our faith. How can we do that?

2. Stay Grounded in Scripture

The Bible is filled with promises and examples of God's unwavering faithfulness. Regularly read and meditate on God's Word, especially passages that resonate with your current situation. Consider the stories of Abraham, Joseph, and David - each of them experienced long delays before God's promises were realised. Reflecting on these accounts can strengthen your faith and remind you that God's timing is perfect.

3. Pray with Perseverance

Prayer is not just about presenting our requests to God; it is also about aligning our hearts with His will. During times of waiting, make prayer a consistent part of your daily life. Pour out your hopes, concerns, and frustrations to God, and ask Him to fortify your faith. Remember, the Holy Spirit helps us in our weakness, interceding for us according to God's will (Romans 8:26-27).

4. Engage with a Supportive Community

Surround yourself with fellow believers who can encourage and uplift you in your faith journey. Share your struggles with trusted friends or mentors who can pray for you and remind you of God's faithfulness. Hearing how others have seen God's promises fulfilled in their lives can renew your faith and give you the strength to keep believing.

5. Speak Words of Faith

The words we speak carry power. Proverbs 18:21 says, *"Death and life are in the power of the tongue."* Even when you do not yet see the fulfilment of God's promises, speak words of faith. Declare God's promises over your life and refuse to give in to doubt. This is not merely positive thinking - it is about aligning your speech with the truth of God's Word, which reinforces your faith.

6. Remember God's Past Faithfulness

Reflect on the times when you have seen God work in your life. Remind yourself of those moments when God has come through for you, even if it was not in the way or timing you expected. Keeping a journal of answered prayers and fulfilled promises can be incredibly encouraging during seasons of waiting. It serves as a tangible reminder that God is faithful and that He will fulfil His promises in His perfect timing.

7. Daily Prayer and Devotion

Staying spiritually grounded during times of waiting is crucial, and the best way to do this is through a consistent routine of prayer, Bible study, and worship. These daily practices help you draw closer to God, keep you in tune with His voice, and give you the grace and patience needed to navigate the waiting period.

8. Begin Your Day with Prayer

Start each morning by setting aside a few moments for prayer. This time allows you to hand over your day to God, seek His guidance, and ask for the strength to trust in His timing. Beginning your day with prayer can set a positive tone, keeping your focus on God's promises, no matter what challenges arise.

9. Engage in Regular Bible Study

Spending time in the Word daily is key to understanding God's character and His promises. Make it a habit to read and reflect on Scripture every day, letting the Holy Spirit speak to you through the Bible. Focus on verses that remind you of God's faithfulness and the value of waiting on Him, such as Psalm 27:14: *"Wait on the Lord; be of good courage, and He shall strengthen your heart; wait, I say, on the Lord!"*

10. Worship with a Thankful Heart

Incorporate worship into your daily routine as a way to express gratitude and trust in God. Whether you sing, listen to worship music, or simply offer praises in your own words, worship shifts your focus from your current situation to God's greatness. It serves as a reminder that He is in control and that His plans for you are good.

11. Keep a Journal of Your Thoughts and Prayers

Journaling can be a powerful practice during the waiting period. Write down your prayers, any Scriptures that speak to you, and the insights you gain during your devotional time. This not only helps you see your spiritual growth but also allows you to look back and recognise how God has been at work in your life.

12. End Your Day with Reflection

Before you sleep, take a moment to reflect on the day. Thank God for His guidance and care and consider any lessons you've learned. This nightly reflection helps you to end your day with peace and prepares your heart to rest, knowing that God's promises remain true, no matter what the day has brought.

13. Overcoming Doubt

It is all too easy for doubt to creep in when we are waiting, especially when the wait feels prolonged. We start to question whether God's promises will ever come to pass, and our faith can begin to waver. Guarding our hearts and minds against this doubt is absolutely crucial.

Consider the Israelites in the wilderness. Despite witnessing incredible miracles, they allowed doubt to take root in their hearts. In Numbers 14:1-4, we read, *"So all the congregation lifted up their voices and cried, and the people wept that night. And all the children of Israel complained against Moses and Aaron... So they said to one another, 'Let us select a leader and return to Egypt.'"* Their lack of faith led them to consider returning to slavery rather than trusting in God's promise of a new land.

God's response was stern. In Numbers 14:26-30, He says, *"How long shall I bear with this evil congregation who complain against Me?... Except for Caleb... and Joshua..., you shall by no means enter the land which I swore I would make you dwell in."* Because of their doubt, an entire generation missed out on the promise.

Discernment and Spiritual Warfare

Delays in the fulfilment of prophecy are not always about timing - they can sometimes be due to spiritual opposition. The Bible gives us clear insight into how spiritual battles can affect the unfolding of God's promises in our lives.

Take Daniel as an example. He had been praying earnestly for understanding, but his answer did not come straight away. In Daniel 10:12-13, an angel finally appears and explains why: *"Do not fear, Daniel, for from the first day that you set your heart to understand, and to humble yourself before your God, your words were heard; and I have come because of your words. But the prince of the kingdom of Persia withstood me twenty-one days; and behold, Michael, one of the chief princes, came to help me, for I had been left alone there with the kings of Persia."*

This passage shows us that Daniel's answer was delayed not because God was slow to respond, but because of spiritual warfare. The angel was held up by a demonic force - referred to as the *"prince of the kingdom of Persia"* - until another angel, Michael, came to assist.

What can we learn from Daniel's situation? Firstly, it is vital to recognise that spiritual opposition is real, and it can play a role in delaying the fulfilment of prophecy in our lives. Secondly, understanding this helps us respond in the right way. So, what can we do in this situation?

8 Things to Do When Facing Spiritual Opposition

1. Discern the Cause of the Delay

Start by asking God for discernment. Not every delay is due to spiritual opposition, but it is crucial to seek wisdom to understand what is really going on. As James 1:5 says, *"If any of you lacks wisdom, let him ask of God, who gives to all liberally and without reproach, and it will be given to him."*

2. Strengthen Your Prayer Life

Like Daniel, persistent prayer is key. When faced with spiritual opposition, you need to respond with consistent and fervent prayer. Ephesians 6:18 encourages us to pray *"always with all prayer and supplication in the Spirit, being watchful to this end with all perseverance."* Keep bringing your requests before God, confident that your prayers are powerful and effective.

3. Engage in Spiritual Warfare

Equip yourself with the full armour of God, as outlined in Ephesians 6:10-18. This includes the belt of truth, the breastplate of righteousness, the gospel of peace, the shield of faith, the helmet of salvation, and the sword of the Spirit, which is the word of God. By standing firm in these spiritual defences, you can resist the enemy's attempts to hinder God's plans in your life.

4. Fast for a Breakthrough

Fasting can be a powerful tool in spiritual warfare. In Matthew 17:21, Jesus said, *"However, this kind does not go out except by prayer and fasting."* Consider adding fasting to your prayer routine when you sense strong spiritual opposition. Fasting sharpens your focus on God and can help break down spiritual barriers.

5. Seek Support from Fellow Believers

Do not try to battle alone. Ask trusted friends, family, or church leaders to join you in prayer. The Bible tells us in Matthew 18:19-20, *"Again I say to you that if two of you agree on earth concerning anything that they ask, it will be done for them by My Father in heaven. For where two or three are gathered together in My name, I am there in the midst of them."* The united prayers of believers can have a powerful effect in overcoming spiritual opposition.

6. Keep Faith and Patience at the Forefront

Spiritual warfare can be exhausting, but it is important to maintain your faith and patience. Hebrews 6:12 advises us, *"That you do not become sluggish, but imitate those who through faith and patience inherit the promises."* Trust that God is with you in the battle and that His promises will be fulfilled in His perfect time.

7. Speak Life Over Your Situation

Declare God's promises over your life and situation. Proverbs 18:21 tells us, *"Death and life are in the power of the tongue."* Speak life and victory over the areas where you feel opposition, affirming God's truth and rejecting any lies from the enemy.

8. Engaging in Spiritual Warfare

When we face delays or obstacles in seeing prophetic words come to fruition, engaging in spiritual warfare becomes crucial. As the apostle Paul advises in Ephesians 6:10-18, we are to *"put on the whole armour of God"* to stand firm against spiritual challenges. This passage highlights the importance of being spiritually equipped to deal with opposition that may hinder the fulfilment of God's promises.

Why Engage in Spiritual Warfare?

Recognising that spiritual opposition can influence the timing and fulfilment of prophecies helps us realise the need for spiritual action. Not every delay is about divine timing; some are due to spiritual forces working against God's plans for us.

Engaging in spiritual warfare strengthens your spirit and helps you stay resolute. By relying on God's power, you reinforce your faith and endurance in the face of challenges. We have been given authority over spiritual forces as believers. Engaging in spiritual warfare allows us to use this authority and counter any opposition to God's purposes.

5 Ways How to Engage in Spiritual Warfare

1. Prayer

Make prayer a cornerstone of your spiritual battle. Ephesians 6:18 urges us to *"pray always with all prayer and supplication in the Spirit."* Consistent and heartfelt prayer aligns you with God's will and invites His intervention. Use prayer to seek guidance, ask for protection, and gain strength to overcome any hurdles.

2. Fasting

Fasting can be a powerful aid in spiritual warfare. It helps you focus on God and shows your earnestness. Jesus mentions the importance of prayer and fasting in Matthew 17:21, saying, *"However, this kind does not go out except by prayer and fasting."* Consider including fasting in your spiritual routine to seek breakthroughs and clarity.

3. Declaration of God's Word

The Word of God is a mighty weapon against spiritual opposition. Ephesians 6:17 describes it as the *"sword of the Spirit, which is the word of God."* Speak Scripture over your situation, declaring God's promises and truths. This practice not only strengthens your faith but also counters the enemy's lies and discouragement.

4. Wearing the Armour of God

Equip yourself daily with the armour of God as outlined in Ephesians 6:10-18:

- **The Belt of Truth:** Anchor yourself in God's truth to fight against deception.

- **The Breastplate of Righteousness:** Guard your heart by living righteously.

- **The Shoes of the Gospel of Peace:** Be ready to spread peace and remain steadfast in trials.

- **The Shield of Faith:** Use faith to block the fiery darts of doubt and fear.

- **The Helmet of Salvation:** Protect your mind with the assurance of salvation.

- **The Sword of the Spirit:** Apply the Word of God in your spiritual battles.

5. Be Vigilant

Stay alert and aware of the spiritual realm. 1 Peter 5:8 advises, *"Be sober, be vigilant; because your adversary the devil walks about like a roaring lion, seeking whom he may devour."* Regularly examine your spiritual state and be ready to defend against any schemes that may arise.

6. Join with Others in Prayer

Engaging in spiritual warfare is often more effective with support from others. Invite trusted believers to pray with you. Matthew 18:19 tells us, *"Again I say to you that if two of you agree on earth concerning anything that they ask, it will be done for them by My Father in heaven."* Collective prayer can enhance your efforts and provide additional support and accountability.

Seeking Wise Counsel

When facing challenges, delays, or uncertainties in the journey of faith, it is essential to seek advice and support from mature believers or spiritual leaders. Proverbs 11:14 reminds us, *"Where there is no counsel, the people fall; but in the multitude of counsellors there is safety."* Wise counsel can be a source of strength, guidance, and encouragement, helping you stay on course when times are tough.

Mature believers and spiritual leaders often have years of experience walking with God. They can offer perspectives you might not have considered, helping you see your situation more clearly. As Proverbs 15:22 says, *"Without counsel, plans go awry, but in the multitude of counsellors they are established."*

Tough times can make you feel isolated or overwhelmed. Having someone to talk to, who understands and can pray with you, provides much-needed support. These trusted individuals can remind you of God's promises and encourage you to keep faith. Seeking counsel can also help you avoid making hasty or unwise decisions. Proverbs 12:15 tells us, *"The way of a fool is right in his own eyes, but he who heeds counsel is wise."* A counsellor can help you discern God's will and guide you away from potential missteps.

6 Things to Do When Seeking Wise Counsel

1. Pray for Guidance in Choosing a Counsellor

Pray that God would lead you to the right person. Look for someone who is spiritually mature, grounded in Scripture, and known for their wisdom and integrity.

2. Be Open and Honest

When you approach a spiritual leader or mature believer for counsel, be open and honest about your situation. Share your concerns, struggles, and the specifics of what you are going through. This transparency allows them to give you the best possible advice.

3. Be Willing to Listen and Learn

It is important to approach counsel with a teachable spirit. James 1:19 advises us to be *"swift to hear, slow to speak, slow to wrath."* Be ready to listen carefully to the advice given, even if it challenges your current thinking.

4. Pray Together

Ask your counsellor to pray with you. Prayer can bring clarity, peace, and a deeper sense of God's presence in your situation. Matthew 18:19 says, *"Again I say to you that if two of you agree on earth concerning anything that they ask, it will be done for them by My Father in heaven."*

5. Take Action on Sound Advice

Once you have received wise counsel, pray over it, and if it aligns with Scripture and God's leading, take action. Proverbs 19:20 encourages us, *"Listen to counsel and receive instruction, that you may be wise in your latter days."*

6. Remain Accountable

Stay in touch with your counsellor or spiritual leader. Share updates on how things are progressing and remain open to further guidance. Accountability can help you stay focused and encouraged as you move forward.

Stay Connected with Your Church Community

During times when you are waiting for a prophetic word to come to pass, it is crucial to stay connected with your church community. Being part of a supportive church family can make all the difference, offering encouragement and practical help when you need it most.

Engaging with your church family provides a steady source of encouragement. Fellow believers can uplift you, pray with you, and share in your journey, helping you remain hopeful and focused.

Staying involved with others helps keep you accountable and committed to your spiritual practices. Regular fellowship encourages you to stay engaged in prayer, Bible study, and other essential disciplines. Your church community can offer valuable insights and advice based on their own experiences. Learning from others who have faced similar challenges can provide fresh perspectives and practical support. You can also receive practical assistance, emotional support, or even just a listening ear. This can be particularly important when you're feeling overwhelmed or discouraged.

6 Ways to Stay Connected With Your Church Community

1. Regular Attendance

Make an effort to attend church services and small group meetings regularly. Hebrews 10:24-25 reminds us to *"consider one another in order to stir up love and good works, not forsaking the assembling of ourselves together, as is the manner of some, but exhorting one another."* Your presence helps build a stronger, more supportive community.

2. Join a Small Group

Getting involved in a small group or Bible study provides a closer-knit environment for building relationships and sharing your journey. These groups offer a supportive space where you can discuss your challenges and receive encouragement.

3. Participate in Church Activities

Take part in church events and activities. Volunteering, attending workshops, or joining ministry teams keeps you engaged and connected with your church family.

4. Reach Out for Support

Do not be afraid to seek support from church leaders or trusted friends within the congregation. Share your struggles, ask for prayer, and seek guidance. Your church community is there to support you.

5. Offer Support to Others

Be proactive in offering support to others who may be facing their own challenges. Providing encouragement and assistance not only strengthens the community but also reinforces your own faith.

6. Stay in Touch

If you cannot attend in person, use digital tools to stay connected. Participate in online services, join virtual prayer meetings, and engage with your church's social media to maintain a sense of community.

Remember, a delay does not mean denial; it is an opportunity for growth, preparation, and deeper trust in God's perfect plan.

Chapter Seven

Living in the Light of Prophecy

As I conclude *What to Do with Prophecy*, it is helpful to remind us of some key terms (the 3Ps) we discussed in chapter one. When we talk about prophets, we are referring to those who deliver God's messages. The prophecies themselves are these messages - divine words spoken to guide, warn, or encourage. Prophesying is simply the act of sharing these messages with others. It is clear that prophecy is not just an ancient practice relegated to the pages of the Bible. Instead, it is a living, dynamic part of our faith that still has a profound impact on our spiritual lives today. From the Old to the New Testament, we see how God uses prophecy to guide, challenge, and encourage His people in both immediate and long-term ways.

In the Old Testament, we often see prophecy as a call to

action, requiring those who receive it to step out in faith and cooperate with God's plan. Take Noah, for example. When God told him about the coming flood, Noah did not just sit back and wait. He spent years building the ark, trusting in God's word even when it seemed impossible (Genesis 6:13-22). Abraham's story is similar. God promised him that he would be the father of many nations (Genesis 17:4-5), but this promise unfolded slowly over time, demanding Abraham's ongoing trust and obedience despite many obstacles.

The Old Testament also shows us moments where God's prophetic word comes to pass without any human effort. When God decided to destroy Sodom and Gomorrah, His warning to Abraham was followed by immediate action. The cities were wiped out swiftly, underscoring God's ability to fulfil His word in an instant (Genesis 18:20-21).

The New Testament continues this theme, offering examples of both instant fulfilment and prophecies that require active human participation. On the one hand, we have stories like that of John the Baptist's birth. When the angel Gabriel told Zechariah that his wife Elizabeth would have a son, the prophecy was fulfilled without delay, with Elizabeth conceiving despite her old age (Luke 1:13, 1:24-25). Similarly, Peter's miraculous escape from prison happened instantly, as an angel led him to freedom without any human help (Acts 12:7-10).

On the other hand, some New Testament prophecies

unfold more gradually, requiring the involvement and cooperation of those who receive them. For example, when Paul gave Timothy prophetic words to encourage and guide him in his ministry (1 Timothy 1:18-19), these were not things that happened overnight. Timothy had to engage with those words, letting them shape his work and his faith over time. Similarly, when the early church received prophetic direction to send out Paul and Barnabas (Acts 13:1-3), it required a period of preparation and action, showing how prophecy can be a process that unfolds as we participate in God's plan.

These examples from both the Old and New Testaments highlight the dual nature of prophecy. Sometimes, God's word comes to pass immediately, showing His power to act decisively and directly. Other times, prophecy requires us to step up and cooperate with God over a longer period, allowing His plans to unfold as we walk in faith and obedience. This balance of immediate and gradual fulfilment reflects the depth of how God interacts with us.

As believers, it is important to approach prophecy with an open heart and a discerning spirit. We need to be ready to embrace God's immediate interventions while also being willing to commit ourselves to the long-term fulfilment of His promises. This means letting prophetic guidance influence our daily choices and actions, helping us to align our lives more closely with God's will.

Peter's words in 2 Peter 1:19 are a fitting reminder for us: "Pay attention to the prophetic message as to a light shining in a dark place, until the day dawns and the morning star rises in your hearts." This captures the essence of prophecy - it is a guiding light that helps us navigate life's challenges, leading us closer to the fulfilment of God's plans.

Prophecy plays a vital and multifaceted role in our faith journey. It connects us with God's purposes, whether those are revealed in an instant or over time. As we continue to seek God's guidance, let us hold on to the prophetic word, allowing it to shape our faith, inspire our actions, and bring us ever closer to the heart of God.

Chapter 8

Testimonies

*O*n Monday morning the 15th of January I joined 60 minutes with God, while the prayer was on going PDSO paused and gave a word of knowledge through the Holy Spirit that "there is someone on this platform you attended a job interview which they said no to you but the Lord is saying that they will change their minds concerning you' I said a big amen.

Behold on the same morning, 8am precisely, whilst I was still sleeping the agency called me and said that the Director has changed his mind. – *CU*

*H*aving bought our flat, it was time to move to a more spacious property. Our mortgage broker applied for the mortgage and we were declined. We changed mortgage brokers and had been trying to secure the mortgage for 5 months. I had initially missed watching 60 minutes with God and decided to *go back to the replay it on Youtube. Whilst watching, PDSO gave a word that there was a lady here who God will do a sudden miracle for and I claimed this word. At around 2pm my broker called and said the bank had approved and sent across our mortgage offer letter. – FR*

I attended an interview last year in October and my interview result was positive, they mentioned I was outstanding so I expected to start immediately but my resumption was delayed. Whilst waiting, I started other jobs, I began working with children who had special needs, whilst I enjoyed my work, the role was quite stressful and toxic, it began to impact my health and I was losing weight. I met with PDSO who prayed for me. God finally came through for me in the nick of time just when I was considering other opportunities, the company called me for the contract. I now work as a senior analyst in Drone Technology, I get to work remotely and my contract has been extended for the third time. - AA

I want to thank God for honouring our act of faith and rebuking the devourer for our sake. We needed to travel by car for an important event however the car developed a fault. Upon taking the car to the mechanic a diagnostic test was done which generated an error code. We received quotes that it could cost over £1000 to fix this fault, also the parts required were either *no longer produced, in stock or could take up to 2-3 working days to arrive. That evening I called on God and anointed the car with oil. I also laid the handkerchief PDSO gave us a while back and declared to the car that it was healed and that we would not need to spend any money on it. The next day God directed us to another mechanic who had a second look. The diagnosis he gave was different and were able to buy the recommended part for less than a tenth of what we thought we needed to spend. The problem was resolved and we were able to travel to where we needed the next day. – **NO***

*There was an incident at my place of work resulting in the death of a patient as a result, all the staff on shift were summoned to face a coroner's investigation. This went on for 2 years, however the day I was to be interviewed by the coroner's panel fell on 60 minutes with God prayers. PDSO said that somebody was going to smile this week and I keyed into that prayer. When it was my turn to be interviewed, all went smoothly. The case was finalised last month and no one lost their job or faced any disciplinary action. – **KJ***

In 2000, I spent a lot of money for my children to come and join me in the UK however all efforts were futile. One day I visited PDSO in his office and he asked after my children, I told him they were in Nigeria. PDSO prayed for me according to

Isaiah 43:5-7 and prophesied that God would bring my children to the UK in a way that would be beyond my imagination. In 2022, I received a call asking me what my plans were of bringing my children to join me in the UK, to which my response was 'I have no money, I am retired'. I was then given a number to call and was helped by a woman of God. To the glory of God, what was costing others thousands of pounds cost me nothing. God broke protocol just for me and by May 2023, my daughter, her husband, their children and my first granddaughter all arrived in the UK to join me. – EA

I want to thank God for the 20-fold Covenants of Royal Connections that are potent over me and my family. PDSO declared that we would be debt free. I claimed it and I believed God because His words always produce results. I disciplined myself to pay off all my embarrassing loans and debts and by God's grace, I am now totally debt free, God made it possible because during this period I never stopped paying my tithe. – Anonymous*

S ometime last year I found a swelling on my sons' body. After taking him to the hospital, we were told he would require a minor surgery. Despite my son feeling fine and experiencing no discomfort from the swelling, I decided to anoint the swelling every night with oil and also placed the handkerchief that PDSO* *gave everyone last year on the area believing God for a miracle according to Acts 19:11-12. God indeed did a miracle and as the swelling disappeared. – **NO***

*I moved to the United Kingdom in September 2022, shortly after the enemy began to attack by matrimonial home of 18 years. Peace eluded my home, which led to a series of troubles, misunderstandings, disagreements and issues. This attack had a direct impact on my spiritual and physical health. In November, I met with PDSO and he prayed with me and anointed me. God helped me to finish the course I was studying excellently well with flying colours and settled my fees in the midst of an unsettled home. By December, things started working out and it was the best Christmas we had experienced. My husband woke me up with a bunch of beautiful fresh flowers and I had never received such before, it seemed like I was dreaming but it was real. God is faithful; indeed, He has turned the captivity of Zion and I am like them that dreamed. – **ML-M***

60 MINUTES
WITH GOD PRAYERS

●LIVE
David Sola Oludoyi
@pastorsolaoludoyi

60 Minutes with God Prayers

Every Monday Morning

5:00am to 6:00am

Convener:
Pastor David Sola Oludoyi
Deputy continental overseer, RCCG Europe